Praise for

Paul exhorts his young protégé, Timothy, to "preach the Word; be prepared in season and out of season; correct, rebuke, and encourage—with great patience and careful instruction" (2 Tim 4:2). Dr. Ken Burge has been preaching the Word for a quarter of a century. He has developed a proven method of sermon preparation, employing the acronym F.I.R.E. Novice and veteran preachers alike will profit from studying Pastor Burge's homiletical approach to Scripture. In this volume, he applies the principles of F.I.R.E. to Paul's letter to the Ephesians, demonstrating how the truths of the book should be communicated.

DR. DOUGLAS LYON, SENIOR PREACHING PASTOR
SHILOH BIBLE CHURCH, BLOOMSBURG, PA

Simplicity and profundity walk hand-in-hand in this highly practical book by Ken Burge. Simplicity is only possible for those who have mastered the material, becoming enabled to understand the profundity of God's Word. Burge presents a practical template (F.I.R.E) for approaching Scripture and follows through with his promise to both model the method and teach the Word.

PAUL SEGER, BIBLICAL MINISTRIES WORLDWIDE

In today's chaotic world, there remains the dual need for the bold exposition of God's Word and discipleship in that Word to transform lives for the glory of God. Pastor Ken Burge takes a wonderful and unique approach in his commentary on Ephesians, bringing together both sound exegesis and practical application through a simple methodology, F.I.R.E., applied to each passage of text. Many commentaries remain in the ivory tower of scholastic study, yet this valuable commentary will help the student, lay teacher, and pastor alike in seeing God's precious Word impressed on both the mind and the heart of those who will hear.

ERIC MOCK, VICE PRESIDENT, SLAVIC GOSPEL ASSOCIATION; PASTOR,
RIVER'S EDGE BIBLE CHURCH

Ephesians on F.I.R.E. is one of those rare gems written for the benefit of those with years of practice in the study of the Word of God and those opening their Bibles for the very first time. Pastor Ken Burge has developed a simple, profound, yet practical method to read, understand, and apply the Word of God. Pastors, lay leaders, as well as people just starting their Christian journey will be able to better understand not only the Epistle to the Ephesians, but also how to apply this method to any other section of Scripture for a deeper study and application of the text to their lives.

ANDY CASTILLO, MISSIONARY TO HONDURAS, WORLD REACH

This book is an outstanding example of inductive Bible study in Ephesians, with care given to accurate interpretation and personal application. Dr. Burge has done excellent work that should be considered by those who desire to study, understand, apply, and teach the truths of Ephesians.

DR. LES LOFQUIST, INTERNATIONAL EXECUTIVE DIRECTOR, IFCA

Ephesians on Fire

EPHESIANS

ON

F.I.R.E.

FAMILIARITY
INTERPRETATION
RELATIONSHIP &
EMPLOYMENT

Dr. Ken J. Burge, Sr.

Deep River
B O O K S

ISBN-13: 9781940269412
ISBN-10: 1940269415

Library of Congress: 2014957663

Cover design by Joe Bailen, Contajus Design

Printed in the United States of America

Dedication

The Almighty led me to Colmar Manor Bible Church in 1977. Little did I know what God planned for me in relation to this ministry. After coming to Jesus through this local assembly just outside of Washington, D.C., God guided me to serve as the Youth Pastor for ten years. He then called me to full-time ministry and I was ordained in 1988 and became the Associate Pastor during that year. By God's grace I received a unanimous vote to become the Senior Pastor in 1991. For over twenty-five years I've been remarkably blessed to be serving in the pastorate to this congregation. It is with a deep sense of awe in God's workings that I dedicate *Ephesians on F.I.R.E.* to my cherished sheep at the Colmar Manor Bible Church.

CONTENTS

INTRODUCTION TO
EPHESIANS ON F.I.R.E.

There was a pastor who had just finished doing premarital counseling for a couple he had consented to marry. He decided to give them a Bible as a wedding gift. He meant to write the Scripture reference *1* John 4:18 on the inside cover. It reads, "There is no fear in love; but perfect love casts out fear, because fear involves torment." Instead he wrote John 4:18. Imagine the newlyweds looking up the reference: "For you have had five husbands, and the one whom you now have is not your husband."

If the right Bible reference is important, how much more the correct interpretation and application of any passage!

Have you ever attempted to know God better by studying His Word? Perhaps you took the plunge financially and purchased a commentary, but felt as you waded through it that you were reading a technical journal specifically written for those who graduated from Harvard—summa cum laude. Maybe you threw up your hands in frustration and prayed, "Lord, direct me to a better way." If so, take heart, dear child of God; this book is designed with you in mind.

Ephesians on F.I.R.E. is an inductive commentary. This simply means that instead of telling you what the Bible teaches, it takes you on the journey to discover its life-changing communication. My goal consists of you learning not only how to derive the meaning of the biblical text before you, but also how to apply the message personally. In other words, my passion includes teaching you how to develop the necessary skill set to become familiar with the Bible passage you are studying, interpret it accurately, relate it to its surrounding contexts, and employ it personally.

F.I.R.E. will be the acronym used for our study. This mnemonic (memory) device stands for familiarity, interpretation, relationship, and employment. We will use all four of these steps each time we travel through a section of Scripture together.

F is the symbol I will use throughout this book to represent *familiarity.* Although I've been privileged to study the Bible at both the undergraduate and graduate levels, with each degree came the emphasis upon "observation" as the first step of Bible study. Doesn't that term seem cold and clinical versus the warmness expressed by "familiarity"? The Word of God shouldn't be placed under the microscope and scrutinized by those wearing white coats in a sterile environment. The origin of the word familiarity derives from the Latin *familiaritas* and means "familiar" or "intimate." Bible study should originate from a deep-seated personal relationship with God.

Interpretation is the second stage of Bible study. Know that when you see the symbol **I** that it stands for interpretation. The technical term for interpretation is hermeneutics, derived from Greek mythology. Hermes, the son of Zeus and Maia, was the messenger god; he was given the task to speak to men from the gods.

Jesus has also sent a messenger or helper to aid the child of God to understand the Scripture. He is the eternal third member of the godhead known as the Holy Spirit. He enlightens our minds concerning God's truth, if we depend upon him. Jesus described the Holy Spirit as "the Spirit of truth" in John 16:13. He personally escorts us in the Bible, as the remainder of the verse says, "He will guide you into all truth."

Relationship is the third phase of our quest to understand the sacred text. The symbol **R** will stand for relationship throughout our travels. I was taught that "correlation" forms the third component in Bible study. Correlation is generally associated with inanimate things while relationship implies a connection between living organisms.

We will see how the life-giving parts ally with the whole. "For the word of God is living and powerful, and sharper than any two-edged sword, piercing even to the division of soul and spirit, and of joints and marrow, and is a discerner of the thoughts and intents of the heart" (Heb. 4:12).

The fourth and final part of this most excellent adventure is *employment.* Look for the symbol **E** to represent "employment," or "application." Application begins when those who have received the living Word are given their authoritative marching orders.

We will then look not only at how those to whom the Bible first came were to respond, but what is required of us today. God designed His Word to transform us into the image of Christ, and that cannot occur without first personally applying it to our lives.

Now that you've been given an introduction to the tools that we will be using, let's embark together upon the Book of Ephesians.

CHAPTER ONE

PAUL'S APOSTOLIC TIDINGS

EPHESIANS 1:1–2

Dr. Bill Bright, founder of Campus Crusade for Christ, often told the story of a famous Texas oil field called Yates Pool: During the Depression this field was a sheep ranch owned by a man named Yates. Mr. Yates wasn't able to make enough on his ranching operation to pay the principal and interest on the mortgage, so he was in danger of losing his ranch. With little money for clothes or food, his family (like many others) had to live on government subsidy.

Day after day, as he grazed his sheep over those rolling West Texas hills, he was no doubt greatly troubled about how he would pay his bills. Then a seismographic crew from an oil company came into the area and told him there might be oil on his land. They asked permission to drill a wildcat well, and he signed a lease contract.

At 1,115 feet they struck a huge oil reserve. The first well came in at 80,000 barrels a day. Many subsequent wells were more than twice as large. In fact, 30 years after the discovery, a government test of one of the wells showed it still had the potential flow of 125,000 barrels of oil a day.

And Mr. Yates owned it all. The day he purchased the land he had received the oil and mineral rights. Yet, he'd been living on relief. He was a multimillionaire living in poverty. The problem? He didn't know the oil was there even though he owned it.[1]

For years Mr. Yates had unwittingly possessed vast resources and yet lived like a pauper! The apostle Paul didn't want the Ephesian believers to mimic this experience spiritually. For this reason he wrote to them this beautifully balanced book.

He addressed in chapters 1:1–3:21 the *placement of the believer*. Consider the elevated status of these Christians based upon two verses in the first half of this epistle. "Blessed be the God and Father of our Lord Jesus Christ, who has blessed us with every spiritual blessing in the heavenly places in Christ" (Eph. 1:3). He builds upon this lofty concept in Ephesians 2:6, "And raised us up together, and made us sit together in the heavenly places in Christ Jesus." In his letter to the Roman church, Paul confirmed why the saints have this privileged status: "and if children, then heirs—heirs of God and joint heirs with Christ" (Rom. 8:17).

Since Paul wrote to local churches in the first century, do his words apply to us today? The answer is a resounding yes. Here's why. The Book of Revelation houses seven letters addressed to the same number of churches (chapters 2–3). To each of the churches—including the first church at Ephesus—the statement is made: "He who has an ear, let him hear what the Spirit says to the churches." Jesus was speaking to everyone—not only each of these seven churches, but to believers today. The modern church needs to heed the eternal Word that was given to the ancient Ephesian church.

In his letter to the Ephesians, Paul progressed from the *placement of the believer* (1:1–3:21) to the *practice of the believer* (Eph. 4:1–6:24). The second half of the book shows that since children of God share the special position of being seated with Jesus in heaven, they are now to apply the revealed truths unveiled in the final three chapters.

Let's now look at Ephesians 1:1–2, Paul's introduction to this prized letter:

Paul, an apostle of Jesus Christ, by the will of God, To the saints who are in Ephesus and faithful in Christ Jesus: Grace to you and peace from God our Father and the Lord Jesus Christ.

NEW KING JAMES VERSION—NKJV

From Paul, chosen by God to be an apostle of Christ Jesus. To God's people who live in Ephesus and are faithful followers of Christ Jesus. I pray that God our Father and our Lord Jesus Christ will be kind to you and will bless you with peace!

CONTEMPORARY ENGLISH VERSION—CEV

PAUL SALUTES THE SAINTS—F

Begin by reading the texts several times. I'd recommend that you also do it out loud. (You will want to follow these steps with every portion of Scripture that is studied.) Approaching the passage reverently, by reading the text with the awe and respect that God's holy Word deserves, facilitates an attitude of learning that pleases the Lord.

Additionally, you will want to formulate pertinent questions from the verses that need answers or clarification in the next two parts of Bible study (interpretation and relationship). Below are my questions:

- Does anything seem unusual to you? For instance, do you customarily introduce yourself at the beginning of correspondence that you write?
- Who is Paul and what does it mean that he's an apostle of Jesus Christ?
- What does the word "saints" mean?
- Where was Ephesus and is there anything significant about that location?
- Why does Paul desire to impart grace and peace from God and the Lord Jesus Christ?

PAUL SALUTES THE SAINTS—I

First-century greetings by epistle-writers occurred at the beginning of the letter, where they would introduce themselves. Our author identified himself as Paul, the apostle.

God selected Paul and set him apart with the designation of apostle. The word "apostle" in the general sense means *one sent with a commission*. In today's terms he would fit the role of an ambassador. An ambassador doesn't operate based upon his own authority but represents the one who sent him.

The apostle Paul didn't volunteer for ministry but was drafted for this office "by the will of God" (see 1 Corinthians 9:1). To be qualified for this apostolic office (in the specific biblical sense of the term) meant that a man must have seen Jesus after his resurrection (Acts 1:22). Paul clearly declared that he was the last individual to have viewed him in person. (Defending Jesus' resurrection in 1 Corinthians 15:8, he stated, "Then last of all He was seen by me also.") I personally believe that Paul was the last Jesus-certified apostle because of his unambiguous claim.

The Lord had entrusted Paul with many specific assignments. One such mission led him to evangelize Ephesus. The name "Ephesus" means *desirable* and the inhabitants could boast about their globally important seaport in the Roman province of Asia. In Paul's day, this attractive city housed approximately a quarter of a million residents. This impressive city featured one of the seven wonders of the ancient world, the massive temple of Artemis (Roman Diana), goddess of fertility.

Paul founded this church during his third missionary journey (Acts 18:23–21:16). He went to the synagogue—his usual practice as he entered every city—and witnessed for three months, followed by a two-year stint in the school of Tyrannus. Sometimes signs and wonders accompanied his preaching (see the next section, "R").

The result of his missionary endeavors in Ephesus consisted of winning converts to Jesus who are called saints. What is a saint? Is it only someone who has been canonized (declared a saint) by church authorities? According to Paul and many others in the New Testament, a saint is any believer, regardless of maturity or holiness.

To the saints in Ephesus, Paul gave his customary greeting, which included a blessing of grace and peace (v. 2). The word "grace" derives from the verb "to rejoice." His wish was to convey God's favor—the meaning of grace—and that produces joy when received. When God imparts his grace or favor to us or through us, he gives that which isn't deserved.

PAUL SALUTES THE SAINTS—R

The Word is dynamically alive in its *relationship* to other passages within and outside of the Book of Ephesians. Let's begin by looking how the first two verses relate to others within the book. In both verse 1 and Ephesians

3:1, the author writes, "I, Paul, the prisoner of Jesus Christ for you Gentiles." Why does he call himself a prisoner? Because he wrote the letter while he was under house arrest in Rome (Acts 28:16–31), when he also may have written letters to the Philippians, Colossians, and Philemon. These four books are often called the prison epistles.

Here Paul extended "grace" to these saints, and in chapter 2 we learn more: God's favor delivered the Ephesians from their sin ("by grace you have been saved") (Eph. 2:5). Further, God's unmerited favor toward believers will be on display "in the ages to come" (v. 7), and "for by grace you have been saved through faith, and that not of yourselves; it is the gift of God" (v. 8).

God not only grants grace to the believer but peace also. The Father through the Son first imparts true peace when you are born again, as Paul states elsewhere: "Therefore, having been justified by faith, we have peace with God through our Lord Jesus Christ" (Rom. 5:1). Contemplate who Jesus is: "For He Himself is our peace" (Eph. 2:14). Now that we have peace with God through Jesus, we must be ready to proclaim him to others. That's why Paul wrote later in his letter to the Ephesians: "And having shod your feet with the preparation of the gospel of peace" (Eph. 6:15).

Peace is given to us once we've believed because the Father has declared us righteous, and Jesus is our peace. The blessed Holy Spirit also came to reside within us when we placed our reliance upon Jesus' death, burial, and resurrection for our salvation. One of the graces that God the Holy Spirit produces in our hearts is peace. It is the third fruit of the Spirit (as recorded in Galatians 5:22). In other words, as we walk with God, we experience his abiding presence that produces peace.

Acts 19 gives us the riveting account of how God worked through Paul by unconventional means to rescue many lost souls in Ephesus. In discussing the relationship between various passages of Scripture, we must draw the connection between his letter to the Ephesians and his experiences among them:

Now God worked unusual miracles by the hands of Paul, so that even handkerchiefs or aprons were brought from his body to the sick, and the diseases left them and the evils spirits went out of them. Then some of the itinerant Jewish exorcists took it upon themselves to call the name of the Lord Jesus over those who had evil spirits, saying, "We adjure you by the Jesus whom Paul preaches." Also there were seven sons of Sceva, a Jewish chief priest, who did so. And the evil spirit answered and said, "Jesus I know, and Paul I know; but who are you?" Then the man in whom the evil spirit was leaped on them, overpowered them, and prevailed against them, so that they fled out of that house naked and wounded. This became known both to all Jews and Greeks dwelling in Ephesus; and fear fell on them all, and the name of the Lord Jesus was magnified. And many who had believed came confessing and telling their deeds. Also, many of those who had practiced magic brought their books together and burned them in the sight of all. And they counted up the value of them, and it totaled fifty thousand pieces of silver. So the word of the Lord grew mightily and prevailed.

ACTS 19:11–20

The unbelieving Ephesians were in the clutches of the wicked one. God intervened through the use of ordinary items from Paul. For instance, his handkerchief (used to wipe the sweat from his body) and his craftsman apron when distributed among the people brought healing and the expulsion of demons. These strange miracles demonstrated Paul's authenticity as an apostle. To the Corinthian church he had earlier proclaimed, "Truly the signs of an apostle were accomplished among you with all perseverance, in signs and wonders and mighty deeds" (2 Cor. 12:12).

Then came the seven sons of Sceva. The response of the evil spirit in the man (from which they had tried deliver him) exposed their unsaved condition. (Have you ever wondered what demons talk about when they roast marshmallows? Verse 15 answers this most hotly debated theological question; the demon declared that he knew who Jesus and Paul were, but— in my modern Ken J. Burge, Sr. [KJB] paraphrase: "Who in tarnation are you guys?")

As a result, many Ephesians came to the faith. Indeed, these recent converts demonstrated genuine repentance by openly confessing their magic formulas and burning their sorcery books. To be sure, God can build a church any way he pleases.

PAUL SALUTES THE SAINTS—E

Let's now see how God's Word was first to be applied by the Ephesians and then to us. Being *employed* means having a job to do. As Christians, God employs us to his holy service. Dear brother or sister, we will never sit in God's unemployment office because we've been called to a lifetime of ministry. Paul saluted the saints in Ephesus, writing, "For we are His workmanship, created in Christ Jesus for good works, which God prepared beforehand that we should walk in them" (Eph. 2:10).

Employing or applying what you've learned from any portion of the Bible is extremely important: "But be doers of the word and not hearers only, deceiving yourselves" (James 1:22). How should Ephesians 1:1–2 be applied by those who originally received this letter, and then also by you and me?

Paul was an apostle; we are ambassadors. He extended grace and peace to the Ephesians. How can we promote God's grace and peace today? Here is your employment, child of God: *Communicate God's favor and peace as his ambassador.*

Contemplate your ambassadorship today and carry the gospel of Jesus Christ as his representative. Ask God to open doors for you wherever you might be. If you work in an office, you could share the good news about Jesus with the person in the cubicle next to you. If you are retired or work out of your home, you might engage a neighbor with the gospel, or as you are running errands, you could give a gospel tract to a bank teller or grocery clerk. Students also have many opportunities to speak with other classmates. The important thing is to deliberately seek occasions to regularly *communicate God's favor and peace as his ambassador.*

Here's why we can do it:

Therefore, if anyone is in Christ, he is a new creation; old things have passed away; behold, all things have become new. Now all things are of God, who has reconciled us to Himself through Jesus Christ, and has given us the ministry of reconciliation, that is, that God was in Christ reconciling the world to Himself, not imputing their trespasses to them, and has committed to us the word of reconciliation. Therefore we are ambassadors for Christ, as though God were pleading through us: we implore you on Christ's behalf, be reconciled to God. For He made Him who knew no sin to be sin for us, that we might become the righteousness of God in Him.

2 COR. 5:17–21

CHAPTER TWO

THREE REASONS WHY YOU SHOULD BLESS GOD

EPHESIANS 1:3–6

⟞⟝

Chuck Swindoll tells the following story of a hospital visit he had made:

The day I arrived to visit, I saw a touching scene. This man had a young son, and during his confinement in the hospital, he had made a little wooden truck for his boy. Since the boy was not allowed to go into the ward and visit his father, an orderly had brought the gift down to the child, who was waiting in front of the hospital with his mother. The father was looking out of a fifth-floor window, watching his son unwrap the gift.

The little boy opened the package, and his eyes got wide when he saw that wonderful little truck. He hugged it to his chest. Meanwhile, the father was walking back and forth waving his arms behind the windowpane, trying to get his son's attention.

The little boy put the truck down and reached up and hugged the orderly and thanked him for the truck. And all the while the frustrated father was trying to say, "It's me, son. I made the truck for you. I gave that to you. Look up here!" I could almost read his lips.

Finally the mother and the orderly turned the boy's attention up to the fifth-floor window. It was then the boy cried, "Daddy! Oh, thank you! I miss you, Daddy! Come home, Daddy. Thank you for my truck." And the father stood in the window with tears pouring down his cheeks.[1]

Brother or sister, where do all our blessings come from? From on high where the eternally exalted God dwells. Envision him standing in heaven, waving his holy arms and saying, "Look up here! I am the source of all your blessings."

While contemplating the Father's love for you, read Ephesians 1:3–6 in two translations:

> Blessed be the God and Father of our Lord Jesus Christ, who has blessed us with every spiritual blessing in the heavenly places in Christ, just as He chose us in Him before the foundation of the world, that we should be holy and without blame before Him in love, having predestined us to adoption as sons by Jesus Christ to Himself, according to the good pleasure of His will, to the praise of the glory of His grace, by which He has made us accepted in the Beloved.
>
> NKJV

> Praise be to the God and Father of our Lord Jesus Christ, who has blessed us in the heavenly realms with every spiritual blessing in Christ, For he chose us in Him before the creation of the world to be holy and blameless in his sight. In love he predestined us to be adopted as his sons through Jesus Christ, in accordance with his pleasure and will—to the praise of his glorious grace, which he has freely given us in the One he loves.
>
> NEW INTERNATIONAL VERSION—NIV

PRAISE GOD FROM WHOM ALL BLESSINGS FLOW—F

Do you remember taking a trip recently? Upon arriving at your location, what did you do first? (No, I'm not referring to checking under your seat cushions for loose change!) You unpacked your luggage. Familiarity marks the first step in unpacking the items in your heavenly suitcase—the text. You begin by respectfully analyzing the contents by asking questions:

- What is the meaning of the word "blessed" (v. 3)?
- Why should you regularly bless God according to that verse?
- Why did God choose me to be his child (v. 4)?
- What does it mean that I was predestined to be adopted by Jesus (v. 5)?
- Who is being referred to as his "Beloved" (v. 6)?

PRAISE GOD FROM WHOM ALL BLESSINGS FLOW—I

Today the profound word, "blessed" has become trite. The expression glides off people's lips without much thought about its rich heritage. How can we offer such pronouncements as "God bless you" with the original and fresh biblical significance they deserve?

The adjective "blessed" begins the third verse and appears again a few words later. It comes from the English verb "bless," used to translate the Greek *eulogeitos,* which had been chosen by the writers of the New Testament to substitute for the Hebrew word *barak,* meaning "to kneel." Our English word "eulogy" originates from this Greek term (*eu* means "good" and *logy* means "word: "good word"). Thus, to bless means to praise or to celebrate with praises, to invoke blessings or good words. God is inherently blessed and worthy of praise. Plainly stated, the Father's essence embodies a permanently blessed condition. Therefore, Paul "eulogizes" him.

Why should we praise the everlasting God? Because, Paul wrote, he has blessed us with endless spiritual blessings. This started happening the instant we put our faith in Jesus for salvation. We enjoy a favored status, "blessed with every spiritual blessing." Three times in one verse Paul used this key word to show that the church's primary blessings are spiritual. (We will see a sampling of them in the relationship section.) By way of contrast, when God lists his potential benefits to Israel in the Old Testament, they are chiefly material (see Deut. 28:1–14). The church of Jesus Christ receives the superior blessings—the spiritual over the material—because Jesus conquered death and ascended to God's right hand. Our nonmaterial treasure trove derives from heaven through our union with Jesus Christ;

God has positioned us there with him. As God's children, he has reserved a place in heaven for each of us because of Jesus' atonement. Jesus secured our heavenly accommodations through His death, resurrection, and ascension (John 14:6).

God has chosen you to be his son or daughter; he picked you for himself. We enjoy a privileged status that we don't deserve. The nineteenth-century London preacher Charles Haddon Spurgeon reportedly said, "God certainly must have chosen me before I came into this world, for he never would have done so afterwards." All of us can relate!

What purpose did God have in choosing us for himself? He selected us as members of His family and to model a life of holiness and integrity, conducted in love (v.4). To practice holiness, one must separate oneself to God while deliberately avoiding sin. The unblemished animal sacrifices of the Old Testament are paralleled by the holiness and integrity of the New Testament saints.

In theological circles you might have heard the word *predestination*. The word means "to be marked out ahead of time." We will study this word further in the next section on relationship. However, a clue to understanding predestination is that it deals with God's *purposes* for the believer. Here in v. 5 we see that God has adopted us to bring himself pleasure or satisfaction according to his will.

When Paul addressed the Ephesians about God's placement services for his children, he was most likely referring to the Roman adoption system. Romans could adopt a male child into their families and give him all the privileges of a natural-born son. God's adoption, mediated through His Son, predestines us into his family with the same spiritual blessings as a full-fledged member of his household. Just think what that means!

Paul's response (v. 6) to God's many blessings to his children is praise. He praised him who "has made us accepted in the Beloved." His expression shows that God has bestowed grace or favor upon us in Jesus Christ. Both here and throughout the Bible, the apostle and many others heap praise upon God for all his wonderful gifts to His children.

PRAISE GOD FROM WHOM ALL BLESSINGS FLOW—R

Let's now see how our text relates to the wider body of Scripture. The adjective "blessed" occurs eight times in the Greek New Testament, in the context of making mention of God. Most refer to the Father and sometimes to the Son: "The God and Father of our Lord Jesus Christ, who is blessed forever..." (2 Cor. 11:31). In Romans 9:5, Jesus is "the eternally blessed God."

What are some of the blessings that come to us from the endless riches of the Godhead? Without comment, let me give several verses from Ephesians where the words "rich" or "riches" appear:

In Him we have redemption through His blood, the forgiveness of sins, according to the riches of His grace.

EPHESIANS 1:7

But God, who is rich in mercy, because of His great love with which He loved us, even when we were dead in trespasses, made us alive together with Christ (by grace you have been saved).

EPHESIANS 2:4–5

To me, who am less than the least of all the saints, this grace was given, that I should preach among the Gentiles the unsearchable riches of Christ.

EPHESIANS 3:8

[Paul praying for the Ephesians]...that He would grant you, according to the riches of His glory, to be strengthened with might through His Spirit in the inner man.

EPHESIANS 3:16

As we begin to conclude the topic of God's rich blessings, consider how he shares with us the resources of his saving grace and mercy. By virtue of this, he gives us the privilege to proclaim him to others (as Paul did) and, because of the "riches of His glory," to pray that God would bring strength to other believers. What a fortune has been handed to us!

Verse 4 brings us to the age-old dilemma: How do you reconcile man's free will and God's election (choosing us to salvation)? I've heard the illustration that before you pass into heaven that there is a sign saying, "Whoever wills may enter," by believing in Jesus (John 3:16). Then once you've gone into heaven, on the other side of the sign it says, "Chosen before the foundation of the world." I think we are supposed to enjoy what God has done for us and rest assured that there are some mysteries that we cannot fully understand on this side of eternity.

However, it isn't a mystery that God requires holy living from his children. God is absolutely holy, and he wants us to be like him: "you shall be holy, for I am holy" (Lev. 11:44). And, "But as He who called you is holy, you also be holy in all your conduct, because it is written, 'Be holy, for I am holy'" (1 Pet. 1:15–16). Our heavenly Father determines the path for our moral compass and compels us to take the high road when it comes to holiness.

Why is practicing holiness so vital for the Christian? The writer of Hebrews answers this: "Pursue peace with all men, and holiness, without which no one will see the Lord" (Heb. 12:14). We cannot know Jesus in a deep and a personal way without practicing holiness. As Jesus said in his Beatitudes, "Blessed are the pure in heart, for they will see God" (Matt. 5:8, NIV).

We must be "without blame before Him in love" (Eph. 1:4), which is like being a flawless sacrificial animal for a burnt offering (Lev. 1:3). (The expression "without blemish" in Ephesians 1:4 is the same Greek word— one word in the Greek but two in English—used in Leviticus 1:3 in the Septuagint, the Greek translation of the Old Testament.) These sacrifices point to the substitutionary sacrifice of the Lamb of God. "For He [God] made Him [Jesus] who knew no sin to be sin for us, that we might become the righteousness of God in Him" (2 Cor. 5:21).

Moving now to verse 5, you will recall the key word I identified with "predestination"—*purpose*. The word "predestined" appears six times in the New Testament. Another of God's purposes in predestination turns up in Ephesians 1:11, which reads, "…in Him [Jesus] also we have obtained an inheritance, being predestined according to the purpose of Him [the Father] who works all things according to the counsel of His will." We have been marked out ahead of time to receive an inheritance from God. That inheritance trumps having a rich uncle!

Furthermore, Romans 8:29 states another purpose of God in predestination—to make us like Jesus: "He also predestined [us] to be conformed to the image of His Son."

We should bless God for lavishing his grace upon us through his beloved Son (v. 6). Praise God, from whom all blessings flow!

PRAISE GOD FROM WHOM ALL BLESSINGS FLOW—E

In Ephesians 1:3–6 we can find three points of action. The first assignment, for the Ephesians and for all of us, is: *Bless God who blesses you through Superman.* Yes, you read it right—Superman. The Latin *super* means "above." Clearly all the rights and privileges granted to you and me exist because of our placement "in Christ." Positionally, we sit with Jesus in the heavenly places.

Plan a praise party! Tomorrow in your devotions include several minutes in which you intentionally bless God, specifically because of how he has favored you. Ask God right now to help you put into practice the words of Hebrews 13:15—"Therefore by Him let us continually offer the sacrifice of praise to God, that is, the fruit of our lips, giving thanks to His name."

The second action point or employment that comes from Ephesians 1:3–4 is this: *Bless God who has chosen you to model him.* You are not only honored to know God intimately; you also possess the astonishing entitlement to show him to others. Write out verse 4 on a 3 x 5 card and determine to memorize it over the next few days. Each time you take out the 3 X 5 card for review, stop and thank God for choosing you to reflect him to those around you. Every believer needs to internalize God's Word; the assimilation of the enduring truths of the Bible helps God's beloved children to form godly patterns.

Employment number three is this: *Bless God who adopted and favors you.* Our heavenly Father has chosen you for his holy aspirations. He has elevated you to the full stature of an adult son; therefore, enjoy your advantages.

Do you think he is delighted when you come to him in prayer? Yep! Plan to bless him during your next prayer time specifically for adopting you and the innumerable kindnesses he's shown toward you. Honor God also by entrusting him with your needs and explicitly sharing your struggles. Follow the admonition of Hebrews 4:16, which reads: "Let us therefore come boldly to the throne of grace, that we may obtain mercy and find grace to help in time of need." He's waiting for you.

CHAPTER THREE

HOW TO LIVE ABOVE YOUR MEANS THROUGH JESUS

EPHESIANS 1:7–12

⸺∿∿⸺

Some children had a beautiful white pet lamb, which someone stole from them and sold to the butcher. The youngsters later discovered that their missing lamb was being led to the slaughter. They passionately pleaded with the butcher to give it back to them. He would not. A gentleman, seeing the grief of the children said, "Give them the lamb: I'll pay for him." The kind man sacrificially paid for the lamb's deliverance. This is redemption. The lamb remained helpless while the children didn't have the means to redeem it, but the compassionate man did. Similarly, Jesus paid the ransom for our redemption.

We enjoy spiritual prosperity not only because of the Father's gracious acts on our behalf, but his intervention through his Son. Verses 7–12 of the first chapter of Ephesians describe our riches based upon what Jesus has accomplished for us:

> In Him we have redemption through His blood, the forgiveness of sins, according to the riches of His grace which He made to abound toward us in all wisdom and prudence, having made known to us the mystery of His will, according to His good pleasure which He purposed in Himself, that in the dispensation of the fullness of the times He might gather together in one all things in Christ, both which are in heaven and which are on earth—in Him, in whom also we have obtained an inheritance, being predestined according to the purpose of Him who works all things according

to the counsel of His will, that we who first trusted in Christ should be to the praise of His glory.

NKJV

In Him we have redemption through His blood, the forgiveness of our trespasses, according to the riches of His grace which He lavished upon us. In all wisdom and insight He made known to us the mystery of His will, according to His kind intention which He purposed in Him with a view to an administration suitable to the fullness of the times, that is, the summing up of all things in Christ, things in the heavens and things on the earth. In Him also we have obtained an inheritance, having been predestined according to His purpose who works all things after the counsel of His will, to the end that we who were the first to hope in Christ would be to the praise of His glory.

NEW AMERICAN STANDARD BIBLE—NASB

LIVING RICH THROUGH JESUS—F

I hope that by now you are getting into the rhythm of walking through a passage using F.I.R.E. Are you ready to develop the fundamental questions that could be derived from your careful reading of the text? Here are mine:

- Who does "In Him" refer to (v. 7)?
- What is the antecedent (a word that points back to another) of "which" (v. 8)?
- How are you to live according to Jesus' redeeming grace (vv. 7–8)?
- What does the word "mystery" mean (v. 9)?
- What does the word "dispensation" mean (v. 10)?
- What is the *purpose* of the "predestination" mentioned (v. 11)?

LIVING RICH THROUGH JESUS—I

Paul began verse 7 with the words "In Him," pointing back to the "Beloved" in verse 6 (Jesus Christ). It is through Jesus Christ that "we have redemption through His blood." By stating "we have," the apostle declares that deliverance belongs to us as a current, continuous possession. God doesn't dangle in front of us our release from sin as a future possibility but sets us free the moment we apply, by faith, the ransom of Jesus' death to our life.

Cults tend to use the incentive program. They have a works-based system that offers salvation contingent upon meeting certain conditions that *may* lead to our future redemption. Not so with Jesus Christ. All of us who have trusted in him can boldly say, "We have redemption through his blood, the forgiveness of sins, according to the riches of his grace."

The word "redemption" means to buy back something or someone, a slave or captive, to set free by paying a ransom. Furthermore, through the blood of Jesus we have the removal of sins because of the vastness of His favor. Only our gracious provider Jesus could secure eternal life for us, and grant us a pardon for our sins.

Jesus didn't just redeem us; he brought us into his intimate counsel. The apostle used the pronoun "which" at the beginning of verse 8; it points back to the word "grace" in the prior verse. This grace literally *overflows* "toward us in all wisdom and prudence." The superabundance of God's grace, based upon his eternal nature, exceeds fixed limits. It produces "wisdom" (knowledge that perceives things as they really are) and "prudence" (discernment that leads to right action).

"Having made known to us the mystery of His will" (v. 9) also testifies to the result of grace without borders. A biblical "mystery" harbors a sacred secret, previously hidden but now revealed. Because the Bible is a progressive revelation, the church knows God's plan personally, through God's disclosure in the New Testament, and this is "according to His good pleasure which He purposed in Himself."

God was well pleased to further unveil "that in the dispensation of the fullness of the times He might gather together in one all things in Christ, both which are in heaven and which are on the earth—in Him" (v. 10).

The word "dispensation" comes from a compound Greek word that means *to arrange a house.* At a future season, God will put all things in order under his authority. (We will learn more about the reason and the timing for all of this under R—relationship.)

The mystery further divulges that another of Jesus' *purposes* in predestination is that "also we have obtained an inheritance" (v.11) through him. The "we" here is contrasted with the "you" of verse 13 and speaks respectively of the Jews. What is the inheritance and when will it be received? (This will also be addressed under R—relationship.)

Finally, all these wonderful gifts are given through Jesus, "that we who first trusted in Christ should be to the praise of His glory" (v. 12). Again, the "we" refers to the Jews. This is determined not only by the contrast of "you" in verse 13 but the "also we" in verse 11, showing a different group than the church (vv. 7–10). God had chosen the Jews to be his special treasure; he expected them to live up to the designation of their name meaning *praise.* Let's talk now about relationship to get a fuller understanding of our text from both inside and outside the Book of Ephesians.

LIVING RICH THROUGH JESUS—R

Why do we need the redemption depicted in the seventh verse? Go back to Ephesians 2:1–2 to find out: "As for you, you were dead in your transgressions and sins, in which you used to live when you followed the ways of this world and of the ruler of the kingdom of the air, the spirit who is now at work in those who are disobedient" (NIV). Succinctly stated, before being redeemed we were spiritually dead and led by Satan.

God's forgiveness of sins (v. 7) goes back to the Jewish celebration of Yom Kippur (the Day of Atonement). The Law required the Jews to fast, and the high priest first offered a sacrifice for himself (Lev. 16:11–14), then he made another sacrifice for the people (Lev. 16:20–28). Another requirement of the Day of Atonement was a scapegoat (Lev. 16:10). The scapegoat driven into the wilderness was a graphic reminder to the children of Israel that their sins were covered for one more year.

How much better the blood of Jesus—who didn't need to first offer a sacrifice for himself—that permanently takes away our sin "according to the riches of His grace."

Do you feel special when someone tells you something in confidence? We know from Ephesians 1:9 that God has taken the church into his confidence: "Having made known to us the mystery of His will, according to His good pleasure which He purposed in Himself." What a marvel—God has revealed the mystery of his will to us, the church of Jesus Christ, including details that nobody ever knew before.

He demonstrated that this was part of his character when he showed Abraham, whom the Scriptures call God's friend, that he was going to destroy Sodom. The Lord deliberated (within the Trinity): "Shall I hide from Abraham what I am doing, since Abraham shall surely become a great and mighty nation, and all the nations of the earth shall be blessed in Him?" (Gen. 18:17–18).

Two thousand years later, Jesus told his disciples, just one day before His death, "You are My friends if you do whatever I command you. No longer do I call you servants, for a servant does not know what his master is doing; but I have called you friends, for all things that I heard from My Father I have made known to you" (John 15:14–15). God seems to delight in self-disclosure to his children. We who live in the church age have had many things revealed to us that even his trusted friend Abraham didn't know. What an honor!

Let's look at verse 10 again before we see how it relates to the rest of the Bible: "...that in the dispensation of the fullness of the times He might gather together in one all things in Christ, both which are in heaven and which are on earth—in Him." To see when "the fullness of the times" comes, we need to step back in time. God created a world that he deemed "was very good," which included the creation of man on the sixth day (Gen. 1:31). Gen. 1:26 recounts the plan for mankind, "Let Us make man in Our image, according to Our likeness; let them have dominion over the fish of the sea, over the birds of the air, and over the cattle, over all the earth and over every creeping thing that creeps on the earth." (The words "Us" and "Our" hint at more than one member in the Godhead.) The Lord not only made man but also gave him the earth to rule over; it was his kingdom.

As we know from Genesis 2, the first couple couldn't match wits with Satan; they were expelled from their paradise (Gen. 3) and the earth was cursed. Death and separation from God (and each other) became the norm. Paul assessed the damage to God's creation in his letter to the Roman church. Personifying creation, he described the devastation that the Fall produced upon the good world that he had made:

> For I consider that the sufferings of this present time are not worthy to be compared with the glory which shall be revealed in us. For the earnest expectation of the creation eagerly waits for the revealing of the sons of God. For the creation was subjected to futility, not willingly, but because of Him who subjected it in hope; because the creation itself also will be delivered from the bondage of corruption into the glorious liberty of the children of God. For we know that the whole creation groans and labors with birth pangs together until now. And not only they, but we also who have the firstfruits of the Spirit, even we ourselves groan within ourselves, eagerly waiting for the adoption, the redemption of our body.
>
> ROM. 8:18–23

When will these things take place? At what time will the inheritance promised in Ephesians 1:11 occur? The Old Testament prophets spoke about a future kingdom. Even Jesus' disciples asked if he would then establish this earthly kingdom before he ascended to the Father (Acts 1:6). But we must wait. At the end of the church age, which began on the day of Pentecost (Acts 2), Jesus will then return to the earth (Rev. 19:11–21) and establish his kingdom upon our planet (Rev. 20). The Messiah will rule as King Jesus. This glorious kingdom will restore paradise to the earth, as the prophet Isaiah wrote in the seventh century before Christ:

> The wolf also shall dwell with the lamb,
> The leopard shall lie down with the young goat,
> The calf and the young lion and the fatlings together;

And a little child shall lead them.
The cow and the bear shall graze;
Their young ones shall lie down together;
And the lion shall eat straw like the ox.
The nursing child shall play by the cobra's hole,
And the weaned child shall put his hand in the viper's den.
They shall not hurt nor destroy in all My holy mountain,
For the earth shall be full of the knowledge of the Lord
As the waters cover the sea. (Isa. 11:6–9)

LIVING RICH THROUGH JESUS—E

How do you live rich through Jesus? You start with the first point of employment: *Live rich through Christ's redeeming grace* (vv. 7–8). The "affluent" Jesus abounds in grace and he has purchased you out of the slave market. You were spiritually dead, held captive by the prince of the power of the air, otherwise known as the Devil. You live rich by appreciating and celebrating your emancipation!

Not only have you been set free, you have been positioned on high with Jesus and granted access to the Father. When times are tough, you can speak to him directly through Jesus and receive assistance: "Let us therefore come boldly to the throne of grace, that we may obtain mercy and find grace to help in time of need" (Heb. 4:16).

Our second point of employment that comes from this passage is: *Live rich through Christ's known will* (vv. 9–10). Although God shared certain truths with his beloved Abraham, the father of faith never saw the day in which we live. He never fully understood how his own willingness to offer up Isaac pointed to God's future sacrifice of his own Son. Even the Old Testament prophets, who prophesied about God's will, never fully understood about Jesus and the implications of his redemption for both Jews and Gentiles. We can live rich as we relish the church's hindsight into God's plans!

Here's how Peter's put it:

Of this salvation the prophets have inquired and searched diligently, who prophesied of the grace that would come to you, searching what, or what manner of time, the Spirit of Christ who was in them was indicating when He testified beforehand the sufferings of Christ and the glories that would follow. To them it was revealed that, not to themselves, but to us they were ministering the things which now have been reported to you through those who have preached the gospel to you by the Holy Spirit sent from heaven—things which angels desire to look into.

PETER 1:10–12

Also, we should daily rejoice that the Father has entrusted to us the totality of his Word. God's unveiled masterpiece, the Bible, has been given to us in its entirety, Genesis to Revelation. The Lord has entrusted to us (the church) a panoramic view through the ages showing that we will be participants in his future kingdom. Just knowing that what lies ahead is secure and that we will personally see Christ establish his future kingdom should cause us to live rich!

Our third employment is tied closely to the second: *Live rich through Christ's inheritance* (vv. 11–12). Of whose last will and testament would you like to be a primary beneficiary? The immense wealth some people may have pales in comparison to the vast resources currently made available to us in Jesus and the innumerable treasures that await us in heaven. We can turn again to Peter for the apostle's insight. He testified that because of Jesus' resurrection we are called "to an inheritance incorruptible and undefiled and that does not fade away, reserved in heaven for you" (1 Pet. 1:4). We have a superior inheritance in Christ because it is eternal, not subject to the decay of the temporal world.

Rejoice that your inheritance from Jesus is not contingent upon the volatility of the stock market or the forces of war. Your eternal windfall is reliable, because the One who promised it to you cannot lie. He enables you to live rich through Christ's inheritance. These are eternal truths.

Chapter Four

God's Mark of Ownership
Ephesians 1:13–14

≈∧≈

In the Burge library reside many books. I love my books! Whenever I purchase a new one—which is quite often—I have a ritual that I always perform. I take out my library book embosser, which a friend gave to me as a gift approximately twenty-five years ago, lift the embosser out of its container, and imprint my *mark of ownership* upon the first page of the new book. It reads: "Library of Kenneth Joseph Burge" with the initials KJB in the middle. This stamp confirms my ownership of the book.

Similarly God placed his stamp of ownership upon you and me at the moment of our conversion. How have we responded to the Embosser's imprint upon our soul? How should we respond? Let's see what Ephesians has to say about this:

> In Him you also trusted, after you heard the word of truth, the gospel of your salvation; in whom also, having believed, you were sealed with the Holy Spirit of promise, who is the guarantee of our inheritance until the redemption of the purchased possession, to the praise of His glory.
>
> Ephesians 1:13–14, NKJV

> And when you heard the word of truth (the gospel of your salvation)—when you believed in Christ—you were marked with the seal of the promised Holy Spirit, who is the down payment of our inheritance, until the redemption of God's own possession, to the praise of his glory.
>
> Ephesians 1:13–14, NET

THE EMBOSSER'S SOUL IMPRINT—F

It is such a delight getting familiar with the contents in the Bible. Let's start by creating our probing questions for Ephesians 1:13–14.

- Who does the "In Him" refer to (v. 13)?
- Why does the NKJV use the word "after" and the NET "when" (v. 13)?
- How are we to be "sealed" and what is the "seal" (v. 13)?
- What does the word "who" (v. 14) point back to?
- How long is the child of God sealed?
- What do the words "to the praise of His glory" teach us?

THE EMBOSSER'S SOUL IMPRINT—I

Paul starts our passage with the words "In Him" (v. 13) that refer to "Christ" (verse 12). He then adds, "you also trusted," which shows that the Gentiles, like the Jews in the Ephesian church, have put their faith in Jesus. Remember that the "we" of verse 12 addressed the Jews while the "you" here in verse 13 focuses upon the Gentiles.

The New King James translation of v. 13 could easily lead an interpreter of Scripture down the wrong theological path. The text reads: "after you heard the word of truth…you were sealed with the Holy Spirit of promise," which sounds like the sealing occurs later than believing did, as if they are two separate acts of grace. If you translate more directly from the Greek, you can see that this is not the case: "In whom also you, having heard the word of the truth, the gospel of your salvation, in whom also having believed you were sealed with the Holy Spirit of the promise."

In other words, there is not a time separation between the believing and sealing, but there is a cause and effect. The cause is "believe" and the effect is "you were sealed." These happen virtually simultaneously.

Continuing in verse 13, "the word of truth" that they heard is further expressed as "the gospel of your salvation." The word "gospel," which means *good news,* appears seventy-seven times in the New Testament, and it first occurs here in Ephesians. When Paul arrived in Ephesus, he had proclaimed "the word of truth, the gospel of your salvation" that these former idol worshippers embraced in order to be saved.

As soon as these previously lost souls believed the life-changing message about Jesus Christ, they were "sealed with the Holy Spirit of promise"— instantaneously. That is to say, the second they placed faith in Jesus, the Embosser of the soul stamped his identifying trademark, the Holy Spirit, within them. "Sealed" refers to an official mark that would have been placed upon a first-century letter to show authenticity and ownership of that correspondence.

Likewise God engraved our souls "with the Holy Spirit of promise" upon our believing the gospel. Why "the Holy Spirit *of promise?*" Because the third member of the Trinity was deposited into our souls as a pledge that God would fulfill his commitment to complete the good work that he had begun in us.

The apostle Paul began verse 14 with the pronoun "who," seamlessly relating it to the Holy Spirit in the previous verse, "who is the guarantee of our inheritance." Have you ever purchased a house? Do you remember what the down payment is called? Money paid to confirm a contract is known as "earnest money." God's Holy Spirit, who seals every believer, becomes the down payment from God to guarantee that he will complete the transaction he has started, assuring our future inheritance.

This word "guarantee" is like an engagement ring. It is a promise of being cared for, for a lifetime. Even today, in Greek the word for engagement ring is the same term ("guarantee") that Paul used in Ephesians 1:14. God has given us a pledge, via the Holy Spirit, that he will come for us in the future and give us our inheritance.

We have been purchased through the shed blood of Jesus Christ, but we have not yet received our inheritance, our final release from sin. Our future inheritance has been pledged to us, and we can be confident that it will be brought to fruition when Jesus returns for us.

Finally, we see here in verse 14 the third instance within a few verses of the words, "to the praise of His glory" (see also verses 6 and 12). This time, it is the Holy Spirit who receives the glorious exultation. He is to be lauded for his sealing ministry that will culminate in our full transformation into the image of Jesus Christ.

Yes! To the praise of his glory!

THE EMBOSSER'S SOUL IMPRINT—R

The Ephesian saints could not have enjoyed the honor of being sealed with the Spirit unless they had first heard the gospel. We learned earlier that the word "gospel" means *good news*. What elements constitute the gospel or good news of God? Let's relate Ephesians 1:13–14 to other passages of the New Testament.

First Corinthians 15:3–4 expresses its essence beautifully: "For I delivered to you first of all that which I also received: that Christ died for our sins according to the Scriptures, and that He was buried, and that He rose again the third day according to the Scriptures." Paul labored diligently to present the gospel of Jesus Christ to all people. He heralded that glorious message to the Corinthians and trumpeted it everywhere he went. Faith in Jesus' death, burial (which proved that he died), and resurrection enables the sinner to become a born-again Christian and to be sealed with the Holy Spirit. Just as Jesus' tomb was sealed, so are we.

Let's examine three aspects of the function of a seal: security, authenticity, and ownership. After Jesus' death and subsequent burial, the official Roman seal with cord and wax would have been placed on the tomb. Any tampering would be easy to ascertain. Matthew reports, "So they made the tomb secure, sealing the stone and setting the guard" (Matt. 27:66). The seal provided security. Of course, it didn't work. Although Rome's security system, including both the seal and armed guards, didn't keep Jesus in the grave, God's seal on our souls is inviolable.

We've seen that God's Holy Spirit seals us securely from the moment we first believe. How long are we safe and sound in the Lord? Paul answered this question later in his letter to the Ephesians: "And do not grieve the Holy Spirit of God, by whom you were sealed for the day of redemption" (Eph. 4:30). The "day of redemption" occurs when Jesus returns for us. God seals us the moment we first believe, and that provision stays with us until death or Jesus returns. The seal testifies to the believer's eternal security. Once we've placed faith in Christ, salvation is ours, and that protection stays with us until we're safely in Jesus' presence. It can be stated: once saved, continuously saved!

The second effect of the Spirit's sealing ministry is heavenly authenticity or approval. When the Lord Jesus had just fed the five thousand (John 6), God the Father authenticated him as his Son and approved him as "the true bread from heaven." We see the confirmatory act in John 6:27, "because God the Father has set His seal on Him." Similarly, God has placed his seal upon you and me, which testifies that we are genuine Christians and have his divine stamp of approval upon our lives.

Third, the sealing of the Holy Spirit implies God's mark of ownership upon us: "…who also has sealed us and given us the Spirit in our hearts as a deposit" (2 Cor. 1:22). Since the Spirit dwells in our hearts as a down payment or earnest, we belong to the one who put the Holy Spirit there in the first place.

Finally, what can we learn about the threefold repetition of the words, "to the praise of the glory" as found within the first chapter of Ephesians? For one thing, the Father (v. 6), the Son (v. 12), and the Holy Spirit (v. 12) are to be exalted impartially for their glorious works. The equality of the Trinity is clearly evidenced by the same acclaim for each member of the Godhead, testifying to parallel status. Paul's praise shows that the Father is God, and the Son is God, and that the Holy Spirit is God. One God in three persons, blessed Trinity.

Their unity can be seen in Jesus' statement that we call the Great Commission: "Go therefore and make disciples of all the nations, baptizing them in the name of the Father and of the Son and of the Holy Spirit" (Matt. 28:19). The baptizing is to be done in "the name," not "the names" of the Father, Son, and Holy Spirit. The singular "name" exemplifies one God in three persons. Praise should be offered to the Father, Son, and Holy Spirit for their incomprehensibly unified work.

THE EMBOSSER'S SOUL IMPRINT—E

We have seen that each member of the Godhead is to be extolled for his ministry role. Perhaps because repetition drives home the point, both points of employment or application originate from this threefold doxology given to the Trinity; each application will focus upon praise.

Employment point number one: *Praise God who sealed your deliverance by the Spirit* (Eph. 1:13). By his Spirit, our gracious Lord shared with us the good news of Jesus' perfectly lived life and substitutionary death for our sins. The Spirit is like John the Baptist, who pointed us to Jesus and said, "Behold! The Lamb of God who takes away the sin of the world" (John 1:29). As soon as we placed our faith in God's Lamb, the Spirit sealed us. This mark of God's ownership upon our lives means that we now possess eternal security in Jesus.

Here's what I want you to do: Sit down and write, in your journal or on a piece of stationery, a thank-you note to the Father, Son, and Spirit, praising them for your secured liberation, and God's mark of ownership on your soul. (Don't put the letter away yet when you finish, because there is more to come.)

Our second point of employment builds upon the first one. It is: *Praise God who secured your inheritance by the Spirit.* "Whoever offers praise glorifies Me" (Ps. 50:23). Continue writing to the Trinity your appreciation for protecting your future heavenly estate through the Holy Spirit's sealing. Specifically thank the triune God for your stored treasures in heaven. In your next prayer time, read your praises aloud to God. Prayer is what we will be looking at in Ephesians 1:15–23, and praise and prayer are a powerful combination.

CHAPTER FIVE

FOUR THINGS TO PRAY FOR EVERY BELIEVER

EPHESIANS 1:15–23

———

A minister, a Boy Scout, and a computer expert were the only passengers on a small plane. The pilot came back to the cabin and hastily explained that the plane was going down but there were only three parachutes and four people. The pilot added, "I should have one of the parachutes because I have a wife and three small children." So he took one and jumped.

The computer whiz said, "I should have one of the parachutes because I am the smartest man in the world and everyone needs me." He took one and jumped.

The minister turned to the Boy Scout and said with a half-smile, "You are young and I have lived a rich life as a Christian, so you take the remaining parachute, and I'll go down with the plane." The Boy Scout said, "Relax Reverend—we still have two parachutes. The smartest man in the world just grabbed my knapsack and jumped out of the plane!"

The humble apostle Paul never would have declared himself the world's smartest man, but he surely deserves recognition as the world's greatest missionary. He understood the importance of humility, and he gave us two prayers in this epistle that show his dependence upon God. Read this first one slowly and reverently:

> Therefore I also, after I heard of your faith in the Lord Jesus and your love for all the saints, do not cease to give thanks for you, making mention of you in my prayers: that the God of our Lord Jesus Christ, the Father of glory, may give to you the spirit of

wisdom and revelation in the knowledge of Him, the eyes of your understanding being enlightened; that you may know what is the hope of His calling, what are the riches of the glory of His inheritance in the saints, and what is the exceeding greatness of His power toward us who believe, according to the working of His mighty power which He worked in Christ when He raised Him from the dead and seated Him at His right hand in the heavenly places, far above all principality and power and might and dominion, and every name that is named, not only in this age but also in that which is to come. And He put all things under His feet, and gave Him to be head over all things to the church, which is His body, the fullness of Him who fills all in all.

EPHESIANS 1:15–23, NKJV

I have heard about your faith in the Lord Jesus and your love for all of God's people. So I never stop being grateful for you, as I mention you in my prayers. I ask the glorious Father and God of our Lord Jesus Christ to give you his Spirit. The Spirit will make you wise and let you understand what it means to know God. My prayer is that light will flood your hearts and that you will understand the hope that was given to you when God chose you. Then you will discover the glorious blessings that will be yours together with all of God's people. I want you to know about the great and mighty power that God has for us followers. It is the same wonderful power he used when he raised Christ from death and let him sit at his right side in heaven. There Christ rules over all forces, authorities, powers, and rulers. He rules over all beings in this world and will rule in the future world as well. God has put all things under the power of Christ, and for the good of the church he has made him the head of everything. The church is Christ's body and is filled with Christ who completely fills everything.

EPHESIANS 1:15–23, CEV

PRAYING FOR LIGHT EYES—F

How can the child of God learn to pray in such a way that connects with the Almighty? We can't transport ourselves back in time and overhear what Jesus prayed when one of his followers asked, "Lord, teach us to pray" (Luke 11:1), but we can study the petitions of the saints as recorded in the Bible. We can also ask questions about the prayer passages in Ephesians, as though we were saying, "Paul, teach us to pray."

- What is the "therefore" (v. 15) there for?
- What does a "spirit of wisdom and revelation" mean (v. 17)?
- Does verse 18 refer to our inheritance or Jesus' inheritance?
- What is the relationship between us and Christ's power, resurrection, and ascension (vv. 19-23)?

PRAYING FOR LIGHT EYES—I

Ephesians 1:15–23 is one long Greek sentence. (Disclaimer on behalf of all English teachers in America: Please don't try this at home!) The "therefore" of v. 15 means "for this reason." What is the "therefore" at the beginning of the text "there for"? To link Paul's prayer to the Father's choosing (v. 4), to the Son's redemption (vv. 7–12), and to the Spirit's sealing (vv. 13–14).

Paul is offering thanksgiving to God for these believers' vertical and horizontal relationships. He did this "After I heard of your faith in the Lord Jesus and your love for all the saints" (v. 15). They had a sincere faith directed toward God in heaven (a vertical gaze). And their belief in God led to an expression of an impartial affection for all their brethren (a horizontal activity).

The word "that" which begins verse 17 gives the first purpose of Paul's thanksgiving and prayer. He calls God "the Father of glory," an expression used only used here in the New Testament, and asked that he "may give you the spirit of wisdom and revelation." Does the "spirit" here mean our human spirit as translated in the NKJV or the "Holy Spirit" as the CEV has it?

The "spirit" seems best understood as a human spirit, as in a godliness of attitude. In other letters, Paul wrote in a similar way. For example: "Shall I come to you with a rod, or in love and a spirit of gentleness?" (1 Cor. 4:21) and, "You who are spiritual restore such a one in the spirit of gentleness" (Gal. 6:1). In addition, the word "spirit" lacks the article "the" before it, which further shows that Paul is probably not referring to the Holy Spirit.

The apostle is praying that the saints in Ephesus would have a "spirit" or disposition of "wisdom" (insight for living) and "revelation" (the unveiling or understanding of who the Father of glory is) "in the knowledge of Him." In Greek, the word translated as "knowledge" conveys the meaning of a *full or complete personal knowledge*. Paul, the ambassador for Christ, greatly desired the Ephesians to have a comprehensive, experiential knowledge of God.

Paul further prayed that "the eyes of your understanding [will be] enlightened that you may know what is the hope of His calling." Literally, he wrote "that the eyes of your heart might have light." The "heart" is the seat of personality, and it needs illumination. The light bulb of God, so to speak, shines on the believer's heart when that individual comprehends his or her heavenly summons. (We will see the implications of this under R— relationship.)

Whereas Ephesians 1:11 stated that Christ is our inheritance, Ephesians 1:18 shows we are Jesus' inheritance. Paul exclaims, "what are the riches of the glory of His inheritance in the saints...." Imagine—our loving God views us as his treasure!

Paul then tried to express the degree of God's awesome power that has been made available for believers (v. 19). He began by introducing the incredible workings of God in the believer by citing the Almighty's "exceeding greatness" (literally, "to cast beyond greatness"). "His power" displays *God's ability* "toward us who believe." It is "according to the working of His mighty power." The Greek word for "working" gives us the English term *energy*. The "mighty power" is literally the "power of His might." Placing these four descriptions of God's ability, energy, power, and might together makes you want to run to your prayer closet and tap into your God-given resources.

The all-powerful God displayed his spiritual muscle "in Christ when He raised Him from the dead and seated Him at His right hand in the heavenly places" (v. 20). Moreover, he governs the universe by His dominion, which includes every angel or demon, not only in this life, but the one to come (v. 21). He has no equals!

The next verse (22) shows that "He [God] put all things under His [Jesus'] feet, and gave Him [Jesus] to be head over all things to the church." To be the "head" means that Jesus rules over the church, "which is His body, the fullness of Him who fills all in all." It is the Lord Jesus Christ who fills His body, the church, with the divine enablements mentioned previously.

PRAYING FOR LIGHT EYES—R

Earlier I mentioned that that Ephesians' had two critical relationships: one was vertical while the other was horizontal (v. 15). Their faith in Jesus expressed the upward belief while their indiscriminate love for the saints displayed a lateral fellowship. Christians truly cannot have one without the other. How do the various aspects of this prayer for the Ephesians relate to other parts of the Bible?

First I think of the challenge the lawyer gave Jesus when he challenged Jesus to specify "the great commandment in the law" (Matt: 22:36). Interestingly the Lord answered the request for a singular great commandment by giving two, but he intertwined them virtually as one: "You shall love the Lord your God with all your heart, with all your soul, and with all your mind. This is the first and great commandment. And the second is like it: You shall love your neighbor as yourself" (Matt. 22:37–39).

The word "like" in verse 39 signifies *to be on a par with*; it indicates *equality*. In other words, the second command is equal to the first. It is easy to say that we love God, but the proof of our love for the invisible God is manifested by our love for our visible neighbor. The apostle of love, John, got at the heart of this matter with a probing question: "But whoever has this world's goods, and sees his brother in need, and shuts up his heart from him, how does the love of God abide in him?" (1 John 3:17). The saints at Ephesus showed their sincere faith in Jesus by loving one another.

Don't you love it when someone practices what he preaches? That's what Paul did. Having written to his children in the faith that he did "not cease to give thanks for you, making mention of you in my prayers" (Eph. 1:16), he also advised the Thessalonians to "pray without ceasing, in everything give thanks, for this is the will of God in Christ Jesus for you" (1 Thess. 5:17–18). No wonder God could entrust Paul with so many churches to shepherd. He could honestly say, "Imitate my thankfulness and prayerfulness."

Paul moved on in verse 18, to pray for his brothers and sisters in Christ to be able to wrap their minds around their call from above. Other biblical writers expressed similar desires for the children of God to understand their divine recruitment, which is a celestial summons (see Hebrews 3:1) and which demands a life of holiness (see 2 Tim. 1:9).

We have been transferred from one kingdom to another and therefore should conduct ourselves accordingly. Consider 1 Thessalonians 2:12, which reads, ". . . walk worthy of God who calls you into His own kingdom and glory." How can we be sure that if we sacrifice to please God now, he'll fulfill in the future what he has promised us? 1 Thess. 5:24 provides the answer: "He who calls you is faithful, who also will do it."

God possesses extraordinary ability that he desires to impart to His children through prayer. That's why Paul encouraged the Ephesian believers later in his letter, in the context of spiritual warfare, "Be strong in the Lord and in the power of His might" (Eph. 6:10). It fascinates me that at the end of the section on the armor of God, the apostle requests prayer for himself that he might boldly preach Christ. Don't miss the connection that the Scripture portrays between prayer and power.

How could the Ephesian saints know God experientially? Additionally, how could they grasp their calling, the idea of being Jesus' inheritance, and the power made available to them? The reasons are stated in verses 20–23. First, Jesus sits at God's right hand ruling over the universe (v. 20). Next, the saints were seated alongside him (Eph. 2:6). Because Jesus is the head of the church (Eph. 1:22), their position "in Christ" (Eph. 1:3) enables them to enjoy these privileges. Finally, Jesus rules over the church and fills it with blessings (Eph. 1:23). No wonder the apostle Paul declared that the Ephesians were wealthy in Christ. We are, too. Get ready to be deployed!

PRAYING FOR LIGHT EYES—E

Paul wrote in 1 Thess. 5:17, "Pray without ceasing." Interestingly, the modifier is placed first in the Greek sentence. Therefore the verse could be translated, "Without ceasing, pray." Stated either way, that is not only a challenging command to obey, but it also leads to a vital question: *How should we pray?*

I've been in pastoral ministry for twenty-five years and personally know the heavy responsibility of caring for a flock. I keep a notebook with the names of my church family listed from A to Z. The alphabetical list is divided equally over five days—Monday through Friday. The two prayers in the Book of Ephesians (the other is in Ephesians 3:14-21) help me to know how to pray regularly for the saints. In Ephesians 1:15–23, Paul gives us four particular things to pray for.

Your employment is to create a list of saints to pray for throughout the week, applying the four points you are about to review. You could list the names of your church family members (if not too many), a Sunday School class that you teach or attend, or any children of God that the Lord lays on your heart. Let's follow the Nike model and "just do it."

First point of employment or prayer engagement: *Pray that believers might know God experientially.* This comes from verse 17 which states, "that the God of our Lord Jesus Christ, the Father of glory, may give to you the spirit of wisdom and revelation in the knowledge of Him." For Paul, everything is about a relationship with the living God, regardless of what difficulties might be presented to him: "That I may know Him and the power of His resurrection, and the fellowship of His sufferings, being conformed to His death" (Phil. 3:10). Fervently pray for those on your list to get up close and personal with the Father.

Secondly, *Pray that believers might know God's calling.* For the Ephesians, Paul asked God that, "the eyes of your understanding being enlightened;...you may know what is the hope of His calling" (v. 18). In Hebrews

3:1 we discovered that we have "the heavenly calling." Jesus understood this very well. When the Devil tempted him (Luke 4) and offered him the kingdoms of this world and their glory, Jesus refused. Nothing could bribe him to forego the cross before going for the crown. He understood that his supernatural calling trumped anything this world's system could offer. Although Satan displayed before Jesus' eyes what this world could offer him, our Lord used his spiritual sight and declined to compromise his calling. Sink your spiritual teeth into Hebrews 4:15–16, "For we do not have a High Priest [Jesus] who cannot sympathize with our weaknesses, but was in all points tempted as we are, yet without sin. Let us therefore come boldly to the throne of grace, that we may obtain mercy and fine grace to help in time of need." Let's pray that other believers will use their spiritual sight to understand this world has nothing of eternal value to furnish them, and that only their heavenly call truly matters!

Moving on, our third point of application is this: *Pray that believers might know God's riches* (v. 18). Satan couldn't entice Jesus even with this world's finest, because Jesus understood God's riches and what awaited him upon the completion of his mission. The writer of the letter to the Hebrews portrays Moses in the same light: "Esteeming the reproach of Christ greater riches than the treasures in Egypt; for he looked to the reward. By faith he forsook Egypt, not fearing the wrath of the king; for he endured as seeing Him who is invisible" (Heb. 11:26–27). Let's pray that our fellow saints might imitate Jesus and Moses and have eyes only for their heavenly riches.

Finally, *Pray that believers might know God's power* (vv. 19–23). Remember that the same dynamic energy that raised Jesus from the dead and enabled him to ascend to God's right hand is available to you, and to those saints for whom you are praying. Ask the Father to reveal the Son's might to those who are registered in heaven who are in your list. Jesus, who is the head of the church and who desires to fill the church with blessing, wants to manifest His life to His followers. Pray hard!

CHAPTER SIX

WHY DID GOD PERFORM THE ULTIMATE DEAD LIFT?

EPHESIANS 2:1–10

⌇⌇⌇

Dr. Erwin Lutzer teaches preaching courses at Trinity Evangelical Divinity School. Every year, he takes his students on a field trip to the local cemetery—so they can preach. He says:

> I take them to a little cemetery in Deerfield, Illinois, and I have them all gather around a certain gravesite. I point out the name, and then I tell one of the students, "Preach the gospel to Mr. Smith here."
>
> They look at me like I'm nuts. So I preach to Mr. Smith with enthusiasm: "Sir, Jesus died for your sins, and you must put your faith in him."
>
> Then I look at the students and tell them, "This is no different than preaching the gospel to unsaved people. The Bible says that they are dead in their sins. You can preach your heart out, but nothing will happen unless God does a miracle to give them the life to listen."[1]

Dr. Lutzer is correct; there is only One who can give life to the spiritually dead. The Spirit-guided apostle wrote to those who were formerly dead, and brought to life, and therefore could be placed positionally in heaven with Jesus:

> And you He made alive, who were dead in trespasses and sins, in which you once walked according to the course of this world,

according to the prince of the power of the air, the spirit who now works in the sons of disobedience, among whom also we all once conducted ourselves in the lusts of our flesh, fulfilling the desires of the flesh and of the mind, and were by nature children of wrath, just as the others.

But God, who is rich in mercy, because of His great love with which He loved us, even when we were dead in trespasses, made us alive together with Christ (by grace you have been saved), and raised us up together, and made us sit together in the heavenly places in Christ Jesus, that in the ages to come He might show the exceeding riches of His grace in His kindness toward us in Christ Jesus. For by grace you have been saved through faith, and that not of yourselves; it is the gift of God, not of works, lest anyone should boast. For we are His workmanship, created in Christ Jesus for good works, which God prepared beforehand that we should walk in them.

EPHESIANS 2:1–10, NKJV

As for you, you were dead in your transgressions and sins, in which you used to live when you followed the ways of this world and the ruler of the kingdom of the air, the spirit who is now at work in those who are disobedient. All of us also lived among them at one time, gratifying the cravings of our sinful nature and following its desires and thoughts. Like the rest, we were by nature objects of wrath. But because of his great love for us, God, who is rich in mercy, made us alive with Christ even when we were dead in transgressions—it is by grace you have been saved. And God raised us up with Christ and seated us with him in the heavenly realms in Christ Jesus, in order that in the coming ages he might show the incomparable riches of his grace, expressed in his kindness to us in Christ Jesus. For it is by grace you have been saved, through faith—and this not from yourselves, it is the gift of God—not by works, so that no one can boast. For we are God's workmanship, created in Christ

Jesus to do good works, which God prepared in advance for us to do.

EPHESIANS 2:1–10, NIV

GOD'S ULTIMATE DEAD LIFT—F

Are you already familiar with the classic text of Ephesians 2:1–10? If so, this will be a great test to see if using F.I.R.E. brings to light and life aspects of this passage that you've never noticed previously. Here we go on another exciting expedition of the Word of God.

- Why does the NKJV have the words, "He made alive" in verse 1, and the NIV translation does not?
- What do the words "in which" in verse 2 point back to?
- Who is "the prince of the power of the air" (v. 2)?
- What is "that not of yourselves" referring to (v. 8)?
- What does it means that we were "created in Christ Jesus unto good works" (v. 10)?

GOD'S ULTIMATE DEAD LIFT—I

The reason the words "He made alive" show up in the NKJV in verse 1 is because they are taken from verse 5, added to smooth out the English translation. Those words didn't appear in Paul's Greek letter to the Ephesians. Have you wondered why I give you two different translations for each passage? Comparing two or more texts should motivate you to ask, "Why are they different?"

My literal Greek translation of verse 1 is as follows: "And you, being dead in the trespasses and the sins." Paul recounted to the saints at Ephesus their walking-dead condition before coming to Jesus. The word "trespasses" means *to fall by the wayside* and "sins" means *to miss the mark*. Paul was not trying to draw a distinction between these two words, but rather combining them for emphasis.

The first two words in verse 2, "in which," refer back to the word "sins" in the previous verse. It was "in their sins" that "you walked according to the course of this world." To "walk" conveys the idea to live or conduct oneself in a particular fashion. "This world" doesn't refer only to the physical earth, but more specifically to *this world's system*.

People can't walk a straight line or swim a direct course if blindfolded. We too, like the Ephesians, have wandered "according to the prince of the power of the air," who is Satan. Our predicament made it impossible for us to walk God's unswerving path because the wicked one had put a blindfold on us. Paul further describes Satan as "the spirit who now works in the sons of disobedience." When we were unsaved, our precarious condition made us walk like marionettes or puppets, with the Devil pulling our strings.

In verse 3, Paul elaborated to the Ephesians (and to us by way of extension) about their wretched spiritual situation before coming to Christ. He wrote, "among whom also we all once conducted ourselves in the lusts of our flesh, fulfilling the desires of the flesh and of the mind, and were by nature children of wrath." There exist no exceptions to this rule; we all behaved similarly.

Thank the Lord for his intervention. We were spiritual goners, "but God who is rich in mercy" came to our rescue (v. 4). Why? With the wonderful nature of a tenderhearted Father, God reached out to humankind through Jesus Christ and gave us what we didn't deserve: his mercy. He liberated us "because of the great love with which He loved us." Even when cataloged among the spiritually dead, led by Satan, and saturated with the filth of this world's system, he manifested two of his greatest attributes toward us: his mercy and his love.

In verse 5, Paul interjected, "even when we were dead in trespasses, [he] made us alive together with Christ (by grace you have been saved)." We share something in common with the Ephesians: Spiritually we used to wear grave clothes, and then God saved us, giving us what we didn't deserve (his grace or favor), and elevating us to stand next to Jesus in heaven.

As a result of God's grace, he "raised up together, and made us sit together in the heavenly places in Christ" (v. 6). Now we can display his achievement. As Ephesians 2:7 puts it, "that in the ages to come He might show the exceeding riches of His grace in His kindness toward us in Christ

Jesus." We will be on exhibit throughout eternity revealing, "the exceeding riches of His grace."

We've already studied that God's favor led to our salvation. However, what vehicle or means did he use to deliver us? Observe verse 8, "For by grace you have been saved through faith." Long ago I heard "faith" defined *as taking God at His Word and acting upon it.* Once you understand that Jesus took your place on the cross (substitutionary atonement), and God raised him from the dead, and you personalize those truths through the medium of faith, you are born again.

What does the word "that" refer to, considering the remainder of verse 8, which reads, "and that not of yourselves?" Does it point back to "grace" or perhaps "faith" in the first part of the verse? In the Greek, the word "that" is neuter, whereas both "grace" and "faith" are feminine; therefore "that" does not refer to "grace" or "faith." It seems that Paul is referring more broadly to the entire process of salvation, not simply pointing toward "grace" or "faith."

Paul then gave more essential information, stating: "It is the gift of God, not of works, lest anyone should boast" (Eph. 2:8b–9). The word for "gift" testifies to the gracious nature of God. Indeed, our salvation doesn't rely upon any human work. This is what sets apart biblical Christianity from all other religions. Other religions depend upon works, whereas Christianity is grace-based, and God's grace immediately brings us into a relationship with the living God.

This awesome portion of Scripture culminates with, "For we are His workmanship, created in Christ Jesus for good works, which God prepared beforehand that we should walk in them." I love the term "workmanship" because the Greek term gives us the English word *poem.* (The ending of the Greek expression for "poem" concludes with the letters "ma," which when added to the root word means *the result of.* Consider yourself the result of a work of God's art or the product of His poem.)

Throughout the New Testament, the word "created" speaks of God's creative energy that produces from nothing (v. 10). We were spiritually dead before Jesus saved us with his power that made all things new. So we've been created from naught, spiritually speaking, "in Christ Jesus for good works, which God prepared beforehand that we should walk in them." We were dangling above hell's fire, and our compassionate heavenly Father snatched us and saved us so that we could live a life of good works that bring glory to his name.

GOD'S ULTIMATE DEAD LIFT—R

There exists nothing good within man that can satisfy a just God; this is the doctrine of "total depravity." We have inherited corruption from Adam (original sin). That is why Ephesians 2:1 depicts us as dead spiritually. God made man in his image (Gen. 1:26), but after Adam disobeyed the Lord in the Garden of Eden, the image suffered corruption and became marred. Ever after, we have been reproducing a marred image (see Gen. 5:3).

Although we are still created in the image of God, that likeness has been damaged. James, speaking about the misuse of the tongue, wrote, "With it we bless our God and Father, and with it we curse men, who have been made in the similitude [likeness] of God" (James 3:9). Jesus came to reverse the pattern, which is why Paul advised the saints, "And be renewed in the spirit of your mind, and that you put on the new man which was created according to God, in righteousness and true holiness" (Eph. 4:23–24).

The Ephesians had once "walked according to the course of this world" (Eph. 2:2), which means that they followed the opposition leader, Satan, "the prince of the power of the air, the spirit who now works in the sons of disobedience." How can you spot the allurements of this world's system, governed by the Prince of Darkness? John wrote about this: "Do not love the world or the things in the world, if anyone loves the world, the love of the Father in not in him. For all that is in the world—the lust of the flesh, the lust of the eyes, and the pride of life—is not of the Father but is of the world. And the world is passing away, and the lust of it; but he who does the will of God abides forever" (1 John 2:15–17).

God extends his mercy to sinners like you and me. Ephesians 2:4 speaks about God's compassion in a striking way: "God, who is rich in mercy." Six centuries earlier, the man known as the weeping prophet (Jeremiah), broken over the plight of Jerusalem and her people, wrote: "It is of the Lord's mercies that we are not consumed" (Lam. 3:22).

The Father not only shares his mercy with us but also his love. Paul marveled at "His great love with which He loved us" (Eph. 2:4), and he praises him for his great generosity: God "made us alive together with Christ…raised us up together, and made us sit together in the heavenly places in Christ Jesus" (vv. 5–6).

Paul wrote another epistle to the Colossian church that parallels many themes in his letter to the Ephesians, showing how our placement with Jesus should affect us now and what impact it will have on our future. "If then you were raised with Christ, seek those things which are above, where Christ is, sitting at the right hand of God. Set your mind on things above, not on things on the earth. For you died, and your life is hidden with Christ in God. When Christ who is our life appears, then you also will appear with Him in glory" (Col. 3:1–4).

Why exactly do we need God's grace for salvation? Adam's transgression has marked every man, woman, and child who has been born into this world. Paul connected the dots in Romans 5:12, "Therefore, just as through one man sin entered the world, and death through sin, and thus death spread to all men, because all sinned." Paul put the verb for "sinned" in the past tense (as he also did in Romans 3:23), because the first man, Adam, stood in our place when he ate the forbidden fruit. When he sinned, we all sinned.

You might say, "That's not fair." But I wonder if I would have done any better. He was created upright and still he disobeyed God. Whether it's fair or not, the fact is that we needed saving. And as Paul wrote to the Roman church: "For the wages of sin is death, but the gift of God is eternal life in Christ Jesus our Lord" (Rom. 6:23).

Now let's look at the last Adam, our second Representative, Jesus. His sacrifice for our sin displayed perfection, which demonstrated God's grace, and brought us a salvation we couldn't earn. "But the free gift is not like the offense. For if by the one man's offense many died, much more the grace of God and the gift by the grace of the one Man, Jesus Christ, abounded to many" (Rom. 5:16). For this reason Paul could write about God's gracious bequest of eternal life, "It is the gift of God, not of works, lest anyone should boast" (Eph. 2:8b–9).

Paul gave a reason for the Ephesians' deliverance in Ephesians 2:10, "For we are His workmanship, created in Christ Jesus for good works." God saved our souls in order for us to serve Him. Our final passage in this section on relationship will show the continuity of salvation followed by good works:

> For the grace of God that brings salvation has appeared to all men, teaching us that denying ungodliness and worldly lusts, we should live soberly, righteously, and godly in the present age, looking for the blessed hope and glorious appearing of our great God and Savior Jesus Christ, who gave Himself for us, that He might redeem us from every lawless deed and purify for Himself His own special people, zealous for good works.
>
> TITUS 2:11–14

GOD'S ULTIMATE DEAD LIFT—E

Our first two employment points give essential information. There are times in the Scripture when the author wants to convey details that the recipients should know, and then calls him or her to action. We have such an example before us. Paul, already writing to believers, wanted to remind them: *You were spiritually dead and led by Satan* (vv. 1–3). Your assignment based upon this first point is to write out your personal testimony with the intent of sharing the gospel.

The apostle Paul often imparted his pre-conversion story with others and then preached Christ. As he stood trial before Agrippa in Acts 26, he testified how he persecuted those who were called Christians (Acts 26:9–12).

At this point, why don't you begin to write a brief account of your life before believing in Jesus. You should emphasize how you were spiritually dead and followed the dictates of your heart and path of this world. Be as specific as possible, but discriminating, in what you intend to share; people do not need to know all of the unsavory details.

Next, our second point of employment: *You were spiritually made alive by God* (vv. 4–9). Commence writing how the Lord led you to himself. This is what Paul did before Agrippa in Acts 26:13–18. "Do a Paul" here. He wove into his personal testimony the gospel message about Jesus' death and resurrection. Make sure to clearly state those elements in what you write. You will want to use 1 Corinthians 15:3–4 as a pattern.

Your third employment point is stated as a command: *Serve God now that you are saved* (v. 10). Do you regularly serve God through your local church? If not, there is no time like the present to begin. To finish your personal testimony, include how your life has changed since coming to Jesus. What are you doing for him? In Acts 26:18, Paul shared what God had called him to: "To open their eyes [of the lost] and to turn them from darkness to light, and from the power of Satan to God, that they may receive forgiveness of sins and an inheritance among those who are sanctified by faith in Me."

Often, believers don't know how to begin witnessing for Jesus. Writing out your personal testimony is a great place to start. Once you've completed it, ask another Christian to allow you to practice sharing your story with him or her, and then humbly receive feedback. This will equip you for the real deal.

I want to greatly encourage you to follow through on this employment, and to put some effort into it. God can use a well-crafted personal testimony in a powerful way. Remember how John spoke of the saints' future triumph over Satan: "And they overcame him by the blood of the Lamb and by the word of their testimony, and they did not love their lives to the death" (Rev. 12:11).

One of the ways that you serve God now that you are saved is by witnessing. Ask God to cultivate a servant's heart within you, a desire to bring glory to the God who rescued you from the clutches of Satan when you were spiritually dead and who gave you the gift of eternal life. I pray this employment will result in seeing many souls come to the faith.

CHAPTER SEVEN

THE NEED TO BUILD ONE BODY FROM ONE BLOOD

EPHESIANS 2:11–22

Let me share a personal story with you that occurred over thirty-five years ago, before I became a Christian. I vividly recall walking down a local street with a few of my buddies when we made eye contact with some young men who lived on the other side of the highway. Both groups had a profound dislike for the other.

Suddenly, the guys who were with me started running at a breakneck pace, and I joined them. I can remember our ringleader glancing at us after we had been running for about a minute and saying, "What are we running from?"

We stopped in the middle of an isolated, dried-up creek bed. It didn't take long for our pursuers to catch up to us. Everyone was panting, and we exchanged glares. Each of the two "alpha males" grasped the shirt of the other. Then, without a word, we went our separate ways.

It grieves me to see a similar pattern of flight on the part of both pastors and parishioners who find themselves in a culturally changing landscape. What are we running from? I pray that the following passage of Scripture will motivate us, as we learn from the early church, to reach the lost and begin to reflect the ethnic diversity in which they minister.

Therefore remember that you, once Gentiles in the flesh—who are called Uncircumcision by what is called the Circumcision made in the flesh by hands—that at that time you were without Christ, being aliens from the commonwealth of Israel and strangers from the covenants of promise, having no hope and without God in the world. But now in Christ Jesus you who once were far off have been made near by the blood of Christ.

For He Himself is our peace, who has made both one, and has broken down the middle wall of division between us, having abolished in His flesh the enmity, that is, the law of commandments contained in ordinances, so as to create in Himself one new man from the two, thus making peace, and that He might reconcile them both to God in one body through the cross, thereby putting to death the enmity. And He came and preached peace to you who were afar off and to those who were near. For through Him we both have access by one Spirit to the Father.

Now, therefore, you are no longer strangers and foreigners, but fellow citizens with the saints and members of the household of God, having been built on the foundation of the apostles and prophets, Jesus Christ Himself being the chief cornerstone, in whom the whole building, being joined together, grows into a holy temple in the Lord, in whom you also are being built together for a habitation of God in the Spirit.

EPHESIANS 2:11–22, NKJV

Therefore remember that formerly you, the Gentiles in the flesh, who are called "Uncircumcision" by the so-called "Circumcision," which is performed in the flesh by human hands—remember that you were at that time separate from Christ, excluded from the commonwealth of Israel, and strangers to the covenants of promise, having no hope and without God in the world. But now in Christ Jesus you who formerly were far off have been brought near by the blood of Christ.

For He Himself is our peace, who made both groups into one and broke down the barrier of the dividing wall, by abolishing in His flesh the enmity, which is the Law of commandments *contained* in ordinances, so that in Himself He might make the two into one new man, thus establishing peace, and might reconcile them both in one body to God through the cross, by it having put to death the enmity. And He came and preached peace to you who were far away, and peace to you those who were near; for through Him we both have access in one Spirit to the Father.

So then you are no longer strangers and aliens, but you are fellow citizens with the saints, and are of God's household, having been built on the foundation of the apostles and prophets, Christ Jesus Himself being the corner stone, in whom the whole building, being fitted together, is growing into a holy temple in the Lord, in whom you also are being built together into a dwelling of God in the Spirit.

EPHESIANS 2:11–22, NASB

THE DEATH THAT KILLS RACISM—F

Let's get familiar with this passage by asking pertinent questions such as these:

- Who are the "Uncircumcision" and "Circumcision" (v. 11)?
- Who is Paul calling "you" in verses 12–13?
- What is the "middle wall of division" (v. 14)?
- Since Jesus was in heaven, how could "He" preach peace to the Ephesians (v. 17)?
- Why does Paul list "apostles and prophets" in that order instead of "prophets and apostles" (v. 20)?
- What is the "whole building" referring to in verse 21?

THE DEATH THAT KILLS RACISM—I

Paul began by commanding the Ephesians to "remember" that prior to salvation they lived like the heathen—"Gentiles in the flesh" (v. 17.) The Jews scorned them with the derogatory label, "Uncircumcision." This ethnic slur was designed to ridicule the Gentiles who didn't enjoy the privileged rite of circumcision, as given to Abraham by God (Gen. 17) as part of His covenant with them.

These Gentiles remained outside God's spiritual loop. "That at that time you were without Christ," wrote Paul (v. 12), and "being aliens from the commonwealth of Israel and strangers from the covenants of promise, having no hope and without God in the world." The apostle is setting the stage to show that the outsiders would become the insiders, solely based upon the intervention of God.

These cut-off heathen not only would be brought into a right relationship with God, but also into a right relationship with the Jewish believers. Verse 14 states, "For He Himself is our peace, who has made both one." Imagine Christ sacrificing His own life to bring reconciliation to the Ephesians, giving them peace with God, and unity with their formerly hostile antagonists. The barrier that had been impassable was now torn down: Jesus "has broken down the middle wall of division between us" (v. 14). In the midst of the Jewish temple, in the court of the Gentiles, stood a wall of stone that had on it these words: "No foreigner may enter within the barrier which surrounds the sanctuary and enclosure. Anyone who is caught doing so will have himself to blame for his ensuing death." Jesus' death opened up the path for the Ephesians to know God personally and to experience equal footing with their Jewish brothers and sisters in Christ.

Jesus had fulfilled the Old Testament Law, providing a way for the hostilities between the Jews and the Greeks to cease. For example, the dietary regulations that would keep the Jews and Greeks apart had been nullified. That's what Ephesians 2:15 implies: "Having abolished in His flesh the enmity, that is, the law of commandments contained in ordinances, so as to create in Himself one new man from the two, thus making peace."

Jew and Gentile had been brought together into one body, the church, through Christ's crucifixion: "...That He might reconcile them both to God in one body through the cross, thereby putting to death the enmity" (Eph. 2:16). As Paul so powerfully proclaimed, through the cross of Jesus and the preaching of that message, both reconciliation and peace had been brought to fruition.

He adds, "And He came and preached peace to you who were afar off and to those who were near" (Eph. 2:17). Not only did Jesus proclaim a message of peace, but so now do his delegates. "He came and preached peace" refers to Jesus heralding peace through his followers.

As a result of the gospel's proclamation, "we both [Jew and Gentile] have access by one Spirit to the Father" (Eph. 2:18). Membership has its privileges. Both parties can draw near to God without encountering any limitation or obstructions. "Now, therefore, you are no longer strangers and foreigners, but fellow citizens with the saints and members of the household of God" (Eph. 2:19). The Ephesian saints were selected for citizenship in heaven and, while still on earth, in the living organization (really a living organism) called the church.

Paul makes it clear that the church has been built on the foundation of "the apostles and prophets" and the chief cornerstone, "Jesus Christ Himself" (v. 14). Notice that Paul didn't reverse the order saying, "the prophets and apostles." If he had done so, he would have been referring to the Old Testament prophets and New Testament apostles, and the church didn't exist in the Old Testament, nor did anyone know that it would exist in the future.

Paul depicted the unity of Jesus' church in verse 21: "In whom the whole building, being joined together, grows into a holy temple in the Lord." He added, "In whom you [Gentiles] also are being built together for a habitation of God in the Spirit." Like the Old Testament temple, the church was, and is, meant to house the holy presence "of God in the Spirit." The apostle marveled that God's presence would dwell in his united people themselves, not within a particular building.

THE DEATH THAT KILLS RACISM—R

Prior to their salvation, the Ephesian saints (who were Gentiles) lived outside of the special blessings that God had imparted to the Jewish people, and they probably watched the Jews at a distance with a certain amount of curiosity. What in particular had the Father done for the Jews? Paul summed it up this way: "...to whom pertain the adoption, the glory, the covenants, the giving of the law, the service of God, and the promises" (Rom. 9:4). God had adopted the nation, had led them by his pillar of cloud and fire, had made various covenants with them, and had given them the Law and many promises. No wonder Paul, in Ephesians 2:11–12, sketched his Gentile-Ephesian audience as being far off from God.

Paul then, using an intensified form of the word "now" in verse 13 for emphasis, exclaimed, "But now in Christ Jesus you who were once far off have been made near by the blood of Christ." Jesus' death removed the barriers that existed between the Jews and the Gentiles. These Gentiles, who had been permitted only limited access to God through the temple, could now immediately draw near to God. In fact, they could tap into blessings that went beyond those enjoyed by the Old Testament Jews.

Do you remember what happened when Jesus died? Matthew 27:51 reports: "And behold, the veil of the temple was torn in two from top to bottom; and the earth quaked, and the rocks were split." Two huge curtains hung in the temple. The first shielded the Holy Place, in which the priests ministered at various times, from outsiders. The second shielded the Holy of Holies, the place where God's presence dwelt. It was this second curtain that was torn—from top to bottom to make clear that this action was God's. Before this only one high priest could enter the Holy of Holies, on one day of the year. The Lord's death opened up the way for both Jew and Gentile—not just one special Jewish man on one set day of the year—to enter God's holy presence.

As in Paul's day, the church of Jesus Christ today should be seeking to bring formerly separated peoples into one body. Let me ask you a touchy question: How many races are there? The biblically correct answer is *one*. There is only one race—the human race. How do I know that? The indisputable answer: The Bible tells me so. When Paul preached to unbelieving Athenians in Acts 17, he stated definitively, "And He has made from one blood every nation of men to dwell on all the face of the earth" (Acts 17:26). We all come from the blood of the first man, Adam. The Lord Jesus also spoke about this, quoting rhetorically from the Book of Genesis: "Have you not read that He who made them at the beginning 'made them male and female?'" (Matt. 19:4).

The first man, Adam, by his one act of disobedience, separated all people from God and instituted disunity between human beings: "Therefore, just as through one man sin entered the world, and death through sin, and thus death spread to all men, because all sinned" (Rom. 5:12). The only way God could restore harmony to the human race was to start again with another Adam: "And so it is written, "The first man Adam became a living being. The last Adam became a life-giving spirit" (1 Cor. 15:45).

Paul described Jesus as the last Adam who could transmit the gift of eternal life to all those who believe: "As was the man of dust, so also are those who are made of dust, and as is the heavenly Man, so also are those who are heavenly. And as we have borne the image of the man of dust, we shall also bear the image of the heavenly Man" (1 Cor. 15:48–49). Because Adam's image was transmitted to us, we received a sin nature that causes separation. Jesus, whose Holy Spirit now dwells within believers, enables us to be right with God and with anyone who has come to Christ, thus creating unity.

Through the ministry of the church I now pastor, I came to know Jesus more than thirty-five years ago. Our community just outside of Washington D.C. was originally mostly Caucasian. Over the years, the population has changed to predominantly African-American, now also with an influx of Hispanics. This defined my goals as a shepherd; reach our town and have our church reflect the diversity of the community.

I knew it would take a movement of the Holy Spirit to accomplish this. I also understood that most likely our church would never be a mega-church. (There are just over four hundred homes in our small town.) I accepted the realities of the ministry that God had graciously granted to me. In part, success for me can be summed up by some of the comments that have come my way over the past few decades from my diverse congregation members.

One African-American friend once commented, "Kenny, if it weren't for you and Kim [my wife], I probably wouldn't like white people." (Did I ever mention that I'm a white guy? Actually I regularly joke with our congregation and remind them that I grew up white!) Another time, she said, "Kenny, I'd take a bullet for you." Not bad from someone who works for the FBI. I take these as compliments, and I believe they are God's way of saying, "Ken (now that I'm older and have a son named Kenny, it's Ken), you are glorifying me because of your love for all people."

The Lord has given me a great love for the Latin world. We were privileged to host an El Salvadoran church in our building for years. It was special getting to know these dear brothers and sisters and to regularly preach to them via a translator. In appreciation for hosting their church, they asked me if I would like them to take me either to the Holy Land or to their native El Salvador. I chose the latter. I must confess that Israel tempted me, but I wanted to experience their culture.

Several years later I made two trips to Honduras to teach homiletics (preaching). We support a missionary named Andy there, and our families have become very close. One time, he paid me a high compliment by saying, "Pastor Ken, you really know how to connect with Hispanics." All my efforts to show the precious saints in Honduras that I truly love them seem to have paid off.

While it may not seem like a great reward to many people, I have come to cherish the priceless relationships I have with my extended family. I'm rich. Through twenty-five years of pastoral ministry, I have been stationed in a good place, and thankfully have not run from change, which has given me a fulfillment that transcends words. In Paul's words, the beauty of it is, "for through Him we both [pick your combination of ethnicities] have access by one Spirit to the Father" (Eph. 2:18).

THE DEATH THAT KILLS RACISM—E

Our first two employment points are like those in the last chapter. Paul's command in verses 11–13 emphasizes the truth that we must exercise our memory: "Therefore remember [thus is an imperative, a command] that you, once Gentiles in the flesh…were without Christ…who once were far off." We should make a point of recalling regularly that our spiritual condition used to be precarious, because we were without Jesus.

Our first employment point is: *Christ's death brings the distant near God* (vv. 11–13). I want you to set aside a few minutes each day for seven days to reflect deliberately upon your former lost condition, and the wonder of now being close to God because of Jesus' death. This is like a "memorial" of sorts. Paul told the Ephesians to remember these things, and we must do the same.

The second employment point should also to be recalled for seven days and practiced in conjunction with the first. I state the second point of application like this: *Christ's death brings unity and access to God* (vv. 14–18). I want you not only to memorialize this truth, but also purpose to pray during this period of time for an individual, family, community, or country with a different skin color than your own. As I observed the changing people groups in my town, I began to pray for them and for our church to be able to reach them.

Along with this, I would also recommend searching your own heart to see if there is any prejudice that needs to be confessed. Think about your family or church heritage, and make things right with God. By so doing, you can help keep wrong thinking from being propagated to the next generation.

Finally, let me give you a third employment point: *Display the glorious unity of Christ's church* (vv. 19–22). I love Paul's terminology about the diverse body of Christ, "in whom the whole building, being joined together, grows into a holy temple in the Lord" (Eph. 2:21). Your task consists of promoting a glorious diverse unity in Jesus' church. Having the right mindset is key to beginning this employment. In other words, you have to want to do this.

You may begin by regularly praying for people of other ethnicities who are in your community, but currently not represented in your church. Ask God to save their souls so that together you can jointly give God glory. Also, your church might have missionaries in various parts of the world who are reaching people who are quite different from the culture of your home church. You could write your missionary a letter in which you share what you have learned in this chapter and how you will commit to pray for his or her outreach.

In conclusion, you might want to talk with your pastor about a strategy to reach the variegated segments in your community. We have personally done all kinds of outreach at my church, Colmar Manor Bible Church. I ran a flag football ministry for years that brought about twenty African American young men into weekly contact with us. During halftime I always gave a devotional that included a gospel presentation. My wife Kim has taught English as a second language to Hispanics, and we have a tutoring ministry that draws in all segments of the population. Ask God what he would prescribe for your church to reach your lost friends with the gospel of Jesus Christ.

CHAPTER EIGHT

THE SACRED SECRET DIVULGED

EPHESIANS 3:1–13

꞊꙰ᴧᴧᴧ꙰꞊

It has been claimed that you can learn a lot in jail—most of it bad—but some good lessons arise in prison. John Bunyan represents one such example. In 1660, he was arrested in England for preaching without a license. While in jail, he started writing his great book *Pilgrim's Progress*. Then more recently we have the Russian, Alexander Solzhenitsyn, who suffered imprisonment for criticizing the Communist party. While being detained, he wrote magnificent poems in his head, which he later published. And you could add Corrie ten Boom to the list. She was detained in a prison camp for trying to save Jews from the Nazis. She lost her family; but she learned that no matter how deep the pit of despair, God's love is deeper.

One more inmate is the apostle Paul, who was arrested and incarcerated in about A.D. 62, and during his detainment he wrote this most helpful letter to the Ephesians. In addition, he also wrote letters to the Philippians, Colossians, and to a disciple called Philemon, all of which survive as books of the New Testament. Since Paul served time (in prison) for the sake of the saints, it behooves us to make time for the sake of what he wrote. Let's get acquainted with Ephesians 3:1–13, to see what God revealed to him:

> For this reason I, Paul, the prisoner of Christ Jesus for you Gentiles—if indeed you have heard of the dispensation of the grace of God which was given to me for you, how that by revelation He made known to me the mystery (as I have briefly written already, by which, when you read, you may understand my knowledge in the mystery of Christ), which in other ages was not made known to the sons of men, as it has now been revealed by the Spirit to His holy apostles and prophets: that the Gentiles should be fellow heirs,

of the same body, and partakers of His promise in Christ through the gospel, of which I became a minister according to the gift of the grace of God given to me by the effective working of His power.

To me, who am less than the least of all the saints, this grace was given, that I should preach among the Gentiles the unsearchable riches of Christ, and to make all see what is the fellowship of the mystery, which from the beginning of the ages has been hidden in God who created all things through Jesus Christ; to the intent that now the manifold wisdom of God might be made known by the church to the principalities and powers in the heavenly places, according to the eternal purpose which He accomplished in Christ Jesus our Lord, in whom we have boldness and access with confidence through faith in Him. Therefore I ask that you do not lose heart at my tribulations for you, which is your glory.

EPHESIANS 3:1–13, NKJV

For this reason I, Paul, the prisoner of Jesus Christ for you Gentiles—if indeed you have heard of the dispensation of the grace of God which was given to me for you, how that by revelation He made known to me the mystery (as I wrote before in a few words, by which, when you read, you may understand my knowledge in the mystery of Christ), which in other ages was not made known to the sons of men, as it has now been revealed by the Spirit to His holy apostles and prophets: that the Gentiles should be fellow heirs, of the same body, and partakers of His promise in Christ through the gospel, of which I became a minister according to the gift of the grace of God given to me by the effective working of his power. To me, who am less than the least of all the saints, this grace was given, that I should preach among the Gentiles the unsearchable riches of Christ, and to make all people see what *is* the fellowship of the mystery, which from the beginning of the ages has been hidden in God who created all things through Christ Jesus; to the intent that now the manifold wisdom of God might be made known by the church to the principalities and powers in the heavenly places, according to the eternal purpose which He accomplished in Christ Jesus our Lord, in whom we have boldness and access with confidence through faith in Him.

Therefore I ask that you do not lose heart at my tribulations for you, which is your glory.

EPHESIANS 3:1–13 (NET)

ONE SECRET WORTH BLABBING—F

Let's ask ourselves some questions about this passage:

- Why did Paul consider himself Jesus' prisoner and not Rome's (v. 1)?
- What is "the mystery" that is spoken about in this section of Scripture?
- Why did Paul respond with such humility when entrusted with the mystery (vv. 8–9)?
- Who are "the principalities and powers in the heavenly places" that learn about "the manifold wisdom of God" (v. 10)?
- What is God's "eternal purpose" (v. 11)?

ONE SECRET WORTH BLABBING—I

Paul began chapter 3 with the words, "For this reason." (Normally we would cover this under relationship, but the interpretation of our passage hinges on these key words.) The exact expression appears again in the beginning of Ephesians 3:14. It is as though Paul heard his chains clanking after writing, "For this reason" in verse 1, and then began an interlude—explaining the purpose of his imprisonment—before resuming his original thought about prayer in verse 14. The words "For this reason" refer back to Ephesians 2:11–22; they point to the melding of both Jew and Gentile into one body.

The apostle started by identifying himself as "the prisoner of Jesus Christ," not the captive of Rome. He understood that in the sovereignty of

God there existed a divine purpose in his imprisonment (one purpose being the writing of this epistle). It was "for you Gentiles" that he was enduring incarceration in Rome, because it truly happened for their advantage.

Prior to this time, God had entrusted him with a "dispensation," or stewardship (v. 2). The term comes from a compound Greek word that means, "the law of the house" or house rule. Paul had been commissioned as the apostle to the Gentiles in order to reach them with the gospel of Jesus Christ. That's why he called it "the dispensation of the grace of God which was given to me for you."

Paul didn't stumble upon this concealed truth; God unveiled it to him. As verse 3 discloses, "He made known to me the mystery." We learned earlier that a "mystery" is a sacred secret, previously hidden, but now revealed. I'll show you later in relationship where this definition came from. We find a clue about the mystery when Paul adds in verse 3, "As I wrote before in a few words," pointing back to Ephesians 2:11–22.

The timing of the revelation of the mystery goes beyond so-called "business as usual." It wasn't known during the Old Testament dispensation, "which in other ages was not made known to the sons of men" (v. 5). The Holy Spirit had disclosed this secret to "His holy apostles and prophets." Again, the word order of "apostles and prophets" importantly draws the distinction that it refers to New Testament apostles and prophets and not the Old Testament prophets and New Testament apostles.

Paul clarified the mystery in verse 6: "...that the Gentiles should be fellow heirs, of the same body, and partakers of His promise in Christ, through the gospel." The apostle also testified that the Jew and Gentile would be incorporated into one body, the church. The word "church" (as used in verse10) means *to call out*, for she didn't exist until the preaching of the apostles and prophets.

Paul was called to trumpet the gospel "according to the gift of the grace of God given to me" (v. 7). God's favor enabled Paul's service (v. 2). The Divine Enabler called Paul to preach "by the effective working of His power." The "effective working" refers to the divine *energy* of "His power." Our English word "dynamite" comes from the term "power."

Paul humbly accepted his calling. He wrote, "To me, who am less than the least of all the saints" (v. 8). The Greek name "Paul" means *small* and this is how the apostle viewed himself, as far inferior to any Christian. The grace of God called him to proclaim "the unsearchable [literally 'not able to track or trace'] riches of Christ." The former persecutor of Christians understood that if he had a thousand lifetimes to search out God's vast treasures, he still wouldn't exhaust them!

He proclaimed God's gospel without discrimination. His vision was "to make all people see what is the fellowship of the mystery" (v. 9). In essence, Jesus told Paul *to shine a light* (the meaning of the word "see") on the mystery. He went on to highlight, "which from the beginning of the ages has been hidden in God who created all things through Jesus Christ."

We should take a moment to ponder the former generations who didn't receive or know about the sacred secret—from Adam to John the Baptist. Paul marveled that the Almighty had designated him to share this precious information with everyone who would listen.

Why had the church received the hand-off concerning the mystery? "To the intent that now the manifold wisdom of God might be made known by the church to the principalities and powers in the heavenly places" (v. 10). The word "manifold," means *many-sided* and the point is that God's wisdom, although on display, is deeper than our minds can grasp.

The "principalities and powers in heavenly places" describe the angels, both good angels and bad angels (called demons), who view God's grace revealed to and proclaimed by the church. These spirit beings witness God's vast plan that has been entrusted to his called-out body, the church. It is an amazing truth: God has chosen you, my brother or sister, as an exhibit to angels, publicizing God's mystery.

Our modeling of this sanctified secret to the spirit realm is "according to the eternal purpose which He accomplished in Christ Jesus our Lord" (v. 11). Only God could have such an elaborate strategy, since before Creation, to display his intent through Jesus. Now, knowing how much he stands for us, "we have boldness and access with confidence through faith in Him" (v. 12). That is, we can with all courage enter God's presence regularly, knowing his eternal plan for us.

The only way a man in prison could request others who are free not to be concerned for him is because he had an eternal perspective based upon the Word of God. The beloved apostle understood that his imprisonment was happening for their betterment. With this in mind Paul could write, "Therefore I ask that you do not lose heart at my tribulations for you, which is your glory" (v. 13).

ONE SECRET WORTH BLABBING—R

There exists a secret worth blabbing: It is God's revealed mystery to Paul (Eph. 3:2). He briefly touched on this in Ephesians 2:11–22. Let's consider our definition of a mystery. It is a sacred secret, previously hidden, but now revealed. We learn from verse 5, "...which in other ages was not made known to the sons of men, as it has now been revealed by the Spirit to His holy apostles and prophets." Prior to God's revelation to the apostles, this concealed truth remained unknown.

Romans 16:25–26 gives us a comprehensive guide to understanding a biblical mystery: "According to the revelation of the mystery kept secret since the world began but now made manifest, and by the prophetic Scriptures made known to all nations, according to the commandment of the everlasting God, for obedience to the faith."

Hints occurred sporadically in the Old Testament that God would bring his grace to the Gentiles. He spoke to Abram (renamed Abraham in Genesis 17): "I will bless those who bless you, And I will curse him who curses you; And in you all the families of the earth shall be blessed" (Gen. 12:3). Exactly how would God bless the Gentiles, who are referred to as "all the families of the earth?" Galatians 3:8 states, "And the Scripture, foreseeing that God would justify the nations [Gentiles] by faith, preached the gospel to Abraham beforehand, saying, 'In you all the nations shall be blessed.'"

Abraham received a foreshadowing of the gospel, but he was not told about the church. Jesus was the first one to speak about the church. When the Lord predicted the birth of the church, he did so with a future tense verb : "I will build My church, and the gates of Hades shall not prevail against it" (Matt. 16:18). Therefore the called-out body, the church, didn't exist in the Old Testament; the apostles and prophets would found the church, which officially was born on Pentecost after Jesus' resurrection (Acts 2).

Just prior to ascending to heaven, Jesus said, "For John truly baptized with water, but you shall be baptized with the Holy Spirit not many days from now" (Acts 1:5). The baptism of the Holy Spirit on the Day of Pentecost (Acts 2) marks the commencement of the church. A key term to associate with baptism is identification. All believers since Pentecost, when coming to Christ, are baptized, or identified, as part of his body, the church.

As Paul testifies in the next chapter of his epistle to the Ephesians, there exists "one Lord, one faith, one baptism" (Eph. 4:5). The "one baptism" pertains to the baptism of the Holy Spirit. Since Pentecost, all children of God become identified with Jesus upon salvation by receiving the Holy Spirit, and simultaneously get placed in the universal church. No time transpires between salvation and the baptizing of the Holy Spirit once faith occurs. This is confirmed when we observe that the Corinthians, who often lacked spiritually, were all nevertheless Spirit-baptized and placed into the church upon coming to Jesus, "For by one Spirit we were all baptized into one body—whether Jews or Greeks, whether slaves or free—and have all been made to drink into one Spirit" (1 Cor. 12:13).

Paul stood amazed that God had called and equipped him for this treasured assignment. Jesus told Ananias about him: "Go, for he is a chosen vessel [literally "a vessel of election"] of Mine to bear My name before Gentiles, kings, and the children of Israel" (Acts 9:15). This follower of Jesus embraced his calling and later described himself as "an apostle of the Gentiles" (Rom. 11:13).

He understood that God had separated him even in his mother's womb to "preach Him among the Gentiles" (Gal. 1:16). Paul felt unworthy of this assignment because he had persecuted the church. This is why he said, "To me, who am less than the least of all the saints, this grace was given, that I should preach among the Gentiles the unsearchable riches of Christ" (Eph. 3:8). In light of his former activity, he wrote "that Christ Jesus came into the world to save sinners, of whom I am chief" (1 Tim. 1:15).

The humble apostle relished the opportunity to shine the floodlight upon the mystery that would be observed "by the church to the principalities and powers in heavenly places" (Eph. 3:10). The words "principalities and powers" occur also in Ephesians 6:12 and refer to demons. (See also 1 Peter 1:12, which speaks of good angels.) Put together, these references show that church-age saints now put the mystery of the church on public display for both good and evil angels.

God has given us a tremendous stewardship responsibility to proclaim the gospel of Jesus Christ and to watch him build his church that consists of both Jews and Gentiles. Not only that, but the angels observe us, the church of Jesus Christ, as we model this beautiful unity of all believers from every ethnic group. This should motivate us to employ what we've learned about this sacred secret.

ONE SECRET WORTH BLABBING—E

Where do you store your most prized possessions? Many people keep them in a secure place like a fireproof box or a safe. And what is your most precious possession of all? The gospel. Therefore our first employment point is, *Treasure the mystery as a sacred trust* (vv. 1–7).

The Christian's best storage bin resides in the heart or mind. On account of this, your first assignment involves memorizing Romans 1:16, which shows the power of the gospel. Learn to value this precious gem: "For I am not ashamed of the gospel of Christ, for it is the power of God to salvation for everyone who believes, for the Jew first and also for the Greek." Cherish the good news of Christ's death and resurrection, because it brings both Jew and Gentile into the church, which is the mystery.

On to your second application point: *Trumpet the mystery and display God's wisdom* (vv. 8–13). Don't forget that you have an audience. Every time you proclaim the gospel of Jesus Christ, the invisible forces of good and evil watch you. You become a placard that testifies of God's eternal plan through the ages.

The angels marvel that God uses sinful people like you and me, who have received God's grace personally, to proclaim and exemplify this glorious mystery to others. As you dwell upon Romans 1:16, develop a courageous spirit to reach a lost world. Remember what Paul told Timothy about doing the work of an evangelist: "For God has not given us a spirit of fear, but of power and of love and of a sound mind" (2 Tim. 1:7).

Our Lord passed down a crystal-clear mission to Paul that has been further entrusted to subsequent generations of the saints. Your assignment is to treasure and trumpet the mystery to display God's wisdom.

I leave you with Paul's doxology that originated from his contemplation of God's magnificent plan for both the church and the nation of Israel:

Oh, the depth of the riches both of wisdom and knowledge of God! How unsearchable are His judgments and His ways past finding out! "For who has known the mind of the Lord? Or who has become His counselor?" Or who has first given to Him and it shall be repaid to him?" For of Him and through Him and to Him are all things, to whom be glory forever. Amen.

ROMANS 11:33–36

CHAPTER NINE

THREE THINGS TO PRAY FOR DISPLAY TO TERRESTRIALS AND CELESTIALS

EPHESIANS 3:14–21

⸺∿∿⸺

Have you ever heard of the disease *Encephalitis lethargica?* The disease attacks the brain and causes people to freeze like a statue, unable to speak or move. Between 1915 and 1926, there was a worldwide epidemic of it. It seems to have died out, although there have been some isolated cases noted.

Today, some Christians seem to have been afflicted with something similar. There are times we freeze like a statue when it comes to our prayer lives. Let's get familiar with our passage in order to "cure prayer freeze."

For this reason I bow my knees to the Father of our Lord Jesus Christ, from whom the whole family in heaven and earth is named, that He would grant you, according to the riches of His glory, to be strengthened with might through His Spirit in the inner man, that Christ may dwell in your hearts through faith; that you, being rooted and grounded in love, may be able to comprehend with all the saints what *is* the width and length and depth and height—to know the love of Christ which passes knowledge; that you may be filled with all the fullness of God. Now to Him who is able to do exceedingly abundantly above all that we ask or think, according to the power that works in us, to Him *be* glory in the church by Christ Jesus throughout all ages, world without end, Amen.

EPHESIANS 3:14–21, NKJV

I kneel in prayer to the Father. All beings in heaven and on earth receive their life from him. God is wonderful and glorious. I pray that his Spirit will make you become strong followers and that Christ will live in your hearts because of your faith. Stand firm and be deeply rooted in his love. I pray that you and all of God's people will understand what is called wide or long or high or deep. I want you to know all about Christ's love, although it is too wonderful to be measured. Then your lives will be filled with all that God is. I pray that Christ Jesus and the church will forever bring praise to God. His power at work in us can do far more than we dare ask or imagine. Amen.

EPHESIANS 3:14–21, CEV

WHAT TO PRAY TO DISPLAY—F

Let's take a closer look at these verses:

- Why does Paul write "For this reason" (v. 14)?
- Who is "the whole family in heaven and on earth" (v. 15)?
- What are God's "riches in glory" as mentioned (v. 16)?
- What does Paul desire the Ephesians to display (vv. 16–19)?
- What does Paul desire the Ephesians to display (v. 20)?
- What does Paul desire the Ephesians to display (v. 21)?

WHAT TO PRAY TO DISPLAY—I

Paul first used the phrase, "For this reason" in Ephesians 3:1, after which came an interlude (vv. 2–13) that further elaborated upon the nature of the mystery given to him. Now he repeats "for this reason" for the second time (v. 14), to continue his original thought. Because he has been entrusted with the mystery that both the Jew and Gentile would comprise the church (Eph. 2:11–22), he launched into his second prayer, and that is why he said, "For this reason I bow my knees to the Father of our Lord Jesus Christ."

Paul built a bridge from verse 14 to verse 15. After he mentioned the Father (v. 14), he connected, "from whom the whole family in heaven and earth is named" (v. 15). The word "family" can be translated as *fatherhood.* All families have their origin in the Father, and in this regard, he is the Father of all. Yet each person individually must believe in Jesus, who then places them into God's family.

Paul began verse 16 with the word "that," which speaks of purpose, writing, "that He would grant you, according to the riches of His glory to be strengthened with might through His Spirit in the inner man." The asking takes place "according to the riches of His glory." God's "glory" is the sum total of His attributes or perfections. What is an attribute or perfection? The attributes or perfections describe the character of God. We will further probe this worthy topic under relationship. Paul had pondered the nature of God and knew that he was able to supply what the Ephesians needed.

In particular, he sought for them "to be strengthened with might through His Spirit in the inner man." Paul prayed that Jesus' body on earth, the church, might develop spiritual muscle. He implored the limitless God to make them mighty in spirit by the power of the Holy Spirit. He does not focus here upon the physical needs of these believers, but rather on their spiritual maturation.

Paul continued, "...that Christ may dwell in your hearts through faith" (v. 17). To "dwell" derives from a compound Greek word where the preposition functions as an intensifier and the verb root means *home.* He entreated Jesus to be fully at home in the Ephesians' hearts. He next used two past perfect tense verbs—which show completed action in past time with the results continuing—"being rooted and grounded in love." The spiritually-minded apostle wanted these believers, who were firmly planted in Christ, to have God's love implanted in them.

The Greek text begins verses 18 and 19 with another purpose clause, which should be translated by "that." The CEV rightly uses "I pray that," whereas the NKJV doesn't use the word "that." The text should say, "That you may be able to comprehend with all the saints what is the width and length and depth and height—to know the love of Christ which passes knowledge; that you may be filled with the fullness of God." The words "may be able" originate from another compound Greek word that uses an intensifier with the verb that means, *to be able* or *strong.* The writer longed for the recipients to fully comprehend the profound love of God, which transcends knowledge, and that God's presence would permeate them!

Nature hates empty spaces—those areas are filled with such things as water and air. God also wants empty spaces filled. Consequently Paul made another request: "...that you may be filled with the fullness of God" (v. 19).

Paul then cites God's capacity to do the impossible: "to Him who is able to do exceedingly abundantly above all that we ask or think, according to the power that works in us" (v. 20). His magnitude is undauntable, even when people dream great things for him to accomplish.

The apostle culminated this prayer with an exclamation of wonder, a doxology: "...to Him be glory in the church by Christ Jesus throughout all ages, world without end, Amen" (v. 21). Paul understood that when his prayers for the church at Ephesus would be answered, God would be praised all the more.

WHAT TO PRAY TO DISPLAY—R

Now we will examine how this portion of Ephesians relates to the broader body of Scripture.

The act of prayer implies that a person solicits something from God on the grounds of his character and competence, and that the person praying is confident that part of God's character is to respond to prayerful requests. His entreaty was launched toward heaven "according to the riches of His glory" (Eph. 3:16). I previously defined God's glory as the sum total of his attributes or perfections. When we consider the attributes of God, as mentioned within the Book of Ephesians and elsewhere in the Bible, we can grasp why the apostle turned to the Almighty for his help.

Two categories of God's attributes are his incommunicable and communicable perfections. "Incommunicable attributes" refer to God's perfections that belong solely to him, which he does not share with us, such as his eternality (God has always existed and will continue to exist forever), unlike us.

Moses wrote about God's eternality: "Lord, You have been our dwelling place in all generations. Before the mountains were brought forth, or ever

You had formed the earth and the world, even from everlasting to everlasting, You are God" (Ps. 90:1–2). Only a timeless God could give the Ephesian believers the things Paul had requested for them. Therefore Paul could pray, "Now to Him who is able to do exceedingly abundantly above all that we ask or think, according to the power that works in us" (Eph. 3:20). God's eternality implies that he has no limitations!

A second incommunicable attribute of God is his immensity. God's presence fills the universe. Aware of God's immensity, Paul could request, "that Christ may dwell in your hearts through faith" (Eph. 3:17). Moreover, because God's presence abounds universally, Paul could pray, "That you may be filled with the fullness of God" (Eph. 3:19).

The second category of God's attributes are his communicable perfections. These attributes belong to God, but he shares them with us. Three such attributes mentioned in Ephesians are his love, mercy, and grace. Not only do these character traits describe our God, but he also graciously imparts them to his children.

Love, mercy, and grace show up in Ephesians 2:4–5, which reads, "But God, who is rich in mercy, because of His great love with which He loved us, even when we were dead in trespasses, made us alive together with Christ (by grace you have been saved.)" All three qualities materialize in conjunction with our salvation, and God's word requires us to practice these virtues.

Let's examine where these perfections pop up elsewhere in Ephesians. Ephesians 4:2 entreats us, "forbearing with one another in love." Then Ephesians 4:15 exhorts us, "speaking the truth in love." And the command is given in Ephesians 5:2 to "walk in love." Not only are we to be dispensers of God's love, but also His favor. Our words should transmit grace. "Let no corrupt communication proceed out of your mouth, but what is good for necessary edification, that it may impart grace to the hearers" (Eph. 4:29).

In addition, God's nature exhibits a fullness of grace and accordingly he bestows his favor upon us. From the very beginning of our letter, grace is mentioned. Paul's greeting of "grace to you" appears in Ephesians 1:2. It is God's grace that saved us (Eph. 2:8). Furthermore, as benefactors of his favor, we will display God's grace throughout eternity (Eph. 2:7).

Moving forward, notice how Paul prays for the Ephesian saints to receive the depth of God's love through Christ: "...that you, being rooted and grounded in love, may be able to comprehend with all the saints what is the width and length and depth and height—to know the love of Christ which passes knowledge" (Eph. 3:17–19). The truth to be embraced is that not only is God love (1 John 4:8), but that he desires us not only to receive it, but also to practice it.

Observe James' sad admonition, "You do not have because you do not ask" (James 4:2). Paul praises the Father and urges us to petition him without limitation, since he "is able to do exceedingly abundantly above all we could ask or think" (Eph. 3:20). He encourages believers to appeal to God to do great things. So does Jesus, in his words to his disciples regarding the fig tree:

> Assuredly, I say to you, if you have faith and do not doubt, you will not only do what was done to the fig tree, but also if you say to this mountain, "Be removed and be cast into the sea," it will be done. And all things, whatever you ask in prayer, believing, you will receive.
>
> MATTHEW 11:21–22

WHAT TO PRAY TO DISPLAY—E

Congratulations! You are a walking billboard. You manifest God's grace publicly "to the principalities and powers in the heavenly places," according to Ephesians 3:10. The context immediately before this second prayer of Paul on behalf of the Ephesians portrays the saints as being a living advertisement concerning the Jew and Gentile becoming one body, the church. He prays there for things that we should also pray for our brothers and sisters in Christ.

The apostle requested for the saints "to be strengthened with might through His Spirit in the inner man" (Eph. 3:16). Paul knew how much this was needed, having been persecuted everywhere he went, and he knew that strength came from the Spirit in the inner man: "Therefore we do not lose heart. Even though our outward man is perishing, yet the inward man is being renewed day by day" (2 Cor. 4:16).

Our first employment point comes from Ephesians 3:16–19, *Pray for the display of God's power*. Request this for yourself personally and for those on your prayer list that you developed from the employment points for Ephesians 1:15–23. Scientists have discovered that the brain has the ability to change itself. Amazingly, Paul wrote nearly two thousand years ago: "…and be renewed in the spirit of your mind" (Eph. 4:23). Memorize this verse, and Romans 12:1–2 as well: "I Beseech you therefore, brethren, by the mercies of God, that you present your bodies a living sacrifice, holy, acceptable to God, which *is* your reasonable service. And do not be conformed to this world, but be transformed by the renewing of your mind, that you may prove what *is* that good and acceptable and perfect will of God."

The renewal of your mind leads to demonstrating the will of God, ". . . that Christ may dwell in your hearts through faith; that you, being rooted and grounded in love, may be able to comprehend with all the saints what *is* the width and length and depth and height—to know the love of Christ which passes knowledge; that you may be filled with all the fullness of God" (Eph. 3:17–19).

Ask God to use his power to touch the inner man of those you are praying for, which will lead to vastly changed lives that display God's strength. Those believers who model Christlikeness to both celestials (angels) and terrestrials (people) will bring glory to God and can attract non-believers to place their faith in Jesus, thus showing God's might.

Your second employment point is, *Pray for the display of God's plan* (v. 20). When an angel appeared to the mother of Jesus, Mary, who was perplexed as to how she could bear the Messiah, queried, "How can this be, since I do not know a man?" Do your remember what the angel told her, using the miraculous conception of Elizabeth as an example? The messenger said, "For with God nothing will be impossible" (Luke 1:37). This is the same as what Paul shared with the church at Ephesus.

Memorize Ephesians 3:20. This verse has challenged me personally on many occasions to ask God for the impossible for the church. Evaluate this question: "Have I limited God in my thinking when it comes to Jesus building his church?" Then, asking God for wisdom, develop some beyond-the-bounds-of-possibility requests, and tenaciously cling to them in prayer.

Pray for the display of God's purpose (v. 21) becomes our third and final application point. Our text reads, "To Him be glory in the church by Christ Jesus throughout all ages, world without end. Amen" (v. 21). Pray for the church of Jesus Christ, that she will bring glory to God. The church of Jesus Christ brings glory to God through the edification of the saints and the evangelization of the lost. Both when we use our gifts to build up the lives of our fellow believers and when we share the gospel with the lost, we offer glory to God. Therefore our goal in prayer should be to ask God to use us to help our brothers and sisters grow spiritually while also reaching out to the lost. Include that specific petition in your next time of prayer.

CHAPTER TEN

UNITED WE STAND, DIVIDED WE BRAWL

EPHESIANS 4:1–6

~~~~~

"The Four Oxen and the Lion" belongs to the collection of *Aesop's Fables*. This following short story packs a powerful punch:

> A lion used to prowl about a field in which four oxen dwelled. Many a time he tried to attack them; but whenever he came near they turned their tails to one another; so that whichever way he approached them he was met by the horns of one of them. At last, however; they fell a-quarrelling among themselves, and each went off to pasture alone in a separate corner of the field. Then the lion attacked them one by one and soon made an end of all four.

Aesop then gave the moral of the story: United we stand, divided we fall.

Aesop's pithy fable brilliantly captures the principle about unity that Paul shared with the Ephesian saints (Eph. 4:1–6). Before we become familiar with our passage, let's review the layout of this masterfully designed epistle. Ephesians 1:1–3:21 dealt with the *placement of the believer*. Paul, the architect of this magnificent literary gem, taught that the saints must first understand their position in Christ before they can apply this second half of the book, which shows the *practice of the believer* (4:1–6:24).

Dear brother or sister, prepare for deployment!

I therefore, the prisoner of the Lord, beseech you to have a walk worthy of the calling with which you were called, with all lowliness and gentleness, with longsuffering, bearing with one another in love, endeavoring to keep the unity of the Spirit in the bond of peace. *There is* one body and one Spirit, just as you were called in one hope of your calling; one Lord, one faith, one baptism; one God and Father of all, who *is* above all, and through all, and in you all.

EPHESIANS 4:1–6, NKJV

As a prisoner for the Lord, then, I urge you to live a life worthy of the calling you have received. Be completely humble and gentle; be patient, bearing with one another in love. Make every effort to keep the unity of the Spirit through the bond of peace. There is one body and one Spirit—just as you were called to one hope when you were called—one Lord, one faith, one baptism; one God and Father of all, who is over all and through all and in all.

EPHESIANS 4:1–6, NIV

PRACTICING THE ONENESS WALK—F

- What is the "therefore" there for (v. 1)?
- What does the word "walk" mean (v. 1)?
- How does a "walk worthy of the calling with which you were called" set the tone for the rest of the Book of Ephesians?
- Why is the word "one" used so often in vv. 4–6?
- What's the meaning of "one Lord, one faith, one baptism" (v. 5)?
- Why are the Father, Son, and Holy Spirit referred to in vv. 4–6?

PRACTICING THE ONENESS WALK—I

The conjunction "therefore" connects Ephesians 4:1–6:24 (the *practice of the believer*) with Ephesians 1:1–3:21 (the *placement of the believer*). The "therefore" links Paul's first three chapters, which explain the teaching of the believer's elevated status in heaven, with the second half of Ephesians (4:1–6:24), which shows how the children of God should lead their lives. Stated otherwise, saints need first to know who they are in Christ (1:1–3:21) and then, based upon that information, they can come to understand how to conduct themselves (4:1–6:24).

After Paul for the second time identified himself as "the prisoner of the Lord" (Eph. 3:1, "the prisoner of Jesus Christ")," he appealed to the Ephesians to "walk worthy of the calling with which you were called" (Eph. 4:1). To "walk worthy" means *to manage oneself properly.* Some scholars believe the word "worthy" conveys the idea of bringing up the two beams of a scale to a horizontal level. In other words, predicated upon their heavenly summons, Paul is recommending that the saints achieve balance between their profession (what they say) and their practice (what they do).

The life of the believer should be lived "with all lowliness and gentleness, with longsuffering" (Eph. 4:2). In secular literature the word for "lowliness" described the Nile River at its low stage. Our posture, based upon our placement in the realm of heaven, should produce humility. "Lowliness" is coupled with "gentleness." "Gentleness" refers to *power under control.* Have you ever seen a western movie where the corralled wild horse needed to be broken? After the horse couldn't throw the rider, it displayed *power under control.* The steed, although still as powerful as before, exhibited tameness.

Both "gentleness" and "longsuffering" appear in Galatians 5:22–23 under Paul's rubric of "the fruit of the Spirit." These graces don't just happen in the lives of the saints; they are by-products of walking with God and allowing the indwelling Holy Spirit to manufacture them. "Longsuffering" Christians possess long fuses. They don't quickly lose their tempers. Our journey toward heaven should be more like a 26.2-mile marathon than a 100-yard dash. We are to be *long to anger,* which means that we manifest an enduring patience.

Paul continued to exhort the Ephesians by "endeavoring to keep the unity of the Spirit in the bond of peace" (Eph. 4:3). "Endeavoring" denotes *diligence* and the present participle shows continually striving to guard the oneness of the Spirit with the "bond" (*vice* or *clamp*) of peace. "Peace" exists when the glue of the Holy Spirit causes believers to be bound together. The apostle encouraged these saints to exert themselves to this end.

Paul then went on to show how the universal church should look to the model of the Trinity for oneness (Eph. 4:4–6). "There is one body" refers to the body of Christ known as the universal church. Although there might be millions of individual local assemblies globally, we are all members of one universal church. Just as there exists one church, there is also only "one Spirit." The Holy Spirit indwells each believer and places us into that one universal body.

The "one Lord" speaks about Jesus Christ and the "one faith" refers to the body of truth revealed in the New Testament (most likely not to our personal faith in Jesus). Paul then closed verse 5 with "one baptism," by which he does not imply water baptism, because that doesn't save anyone, but Spirit baptism. When someone places faith in Jesus, the Holy Spirit immediately baptizes him or her into the body of Christ, the church.

Ephesians 4:6 closes Paul's paragraph about unity with, "One God and Father of all, who is above all, and through all, and in you all." The four "alls" express that God is the Father of every believer and he rules over everyone and works in each saint and also lives in every Christian. Our Three-in-One God not only displays oneness but also calls us to do the same.

PRACTICING THE ONENESS WALK—R

Paul had a lot to say in this small epistle about the believer's conduct, or walk with Christ. The word "walk" is used eight times in the Book of Ephesians. It occurs six times within chapters 4 through 6.

This key term appears both negatively and positively. Ephesians 4:17 uses the expression negatively, twice: "This I say, therefore, and testify in the Lord, that you should no longer walk as the rest of the Gentiles walk, in the futility of their mind." Paul didn't want the saints imitating the vain practices of the unsaved.

Then the verb surfaces three times as an imperative, each time in the present tense showing continuous action. The first command emerges in

Ephesians 5:2, and states, "Walk in love." The apostle then moves from love to light in Ephesians 5:8, where he directed, "Walk as children of light." Third, he offered, "Walk circumspectly" (Eph. 5:15), which means living one's life carefully in order to please God. Combining all of these, believers are charged to walk in humility, in love, abiding in the light, living diligently in obedience to the Lord.

The Ephesians were "to walk worthy of the calling with which you were called." God had called these saints from his heavenly abode and placed high expectations upon them. First Thessalonians 2:12 begins with a Greek construction that speaks of purpose. It reads, "…that [purpose] you would have a walk worthy of God who calls you into His own kingdom and glory." Since we have been transferred from the kingdom of darkness into the kingdom of light, God purposes that our Christian conduct should reflect our celestial calling.

The Father's call requires us to live "with all lowliness and gentleness" (Eph. 4:2). "Lowliness" means *with humility* and that is how the Greek word is translated in 1 Peter 5:5—"Likewise you younger people, submit yourselves to your elders. Yes, all of you be submissive to one another and be clothed with humility [or "lowliness"], for God resists the proud, but gives grace to the humble."

Speaking about "the humble," remember that there was no meeker man than Moses in his generation. Our word "gentleness" in the Greek translation of the Old Testament that is called the Septuagint gives us the English word "humble": "Now the man Moses *was* very humble [like "gentleness" in Ephesians 4:2], more than all men who were on the face of the earth" (Num. 12:3). We have been called to display in our lives the same humbleness that Moses did.

The character traits listed in Ephesians 4:2 are essential for preserving oneness in the body of Christ. Paul was seeking this unity for those at Ephesus when he wrote: "…endeavoring to keep the unity of the Spirit in the bond of peace" (Eph. 4:3). Peace isn't always possible, even in the church, but it must be pursued. "If it is possible," wrote Paul to the church in Rome, "as much as depends on you, live peaceably with all men" (Rom. 12:18). If this is important for the saints to live peaceably with all men, including the lost, how much more necessary is it for them to strive for this peace within the church of Jesus Christ?

Paul used the word "one" seven times in Ephesians 4:4–6, because of the example of unity for the church that is displayed by the Trinity. He began by saying, "There is one body," (described in Eph. 2:11–22). He then spoke about the oneness of the Spirit, "just as you were called in one hope of your calling" (Eph. 4:4). The "one hope" Paul addressed refers to the rapture, as he also used it in Titus 2:13, where he wrote, "…looking for the blessed hope, and the glorious appearing of our great God and Savior Jesus Christ." Jesus is called not only "our great God" but also "the blessed hope."

Moving on to Ephesians 4:5, we read the words, "…one Lord, one faith, one baptism." Only Jesus is the true God and the "one faith" recalls that great body of truth unveiled in the New Testament. Consider how Jude 3 uses "faith" not as our personal faith but the body of truth as now disclosed in the Bible. "I found it necessary to write to you exhorting you to contend earnestly for the faith [the gospel and revealed New Testament truth] which was once for all delivered to the saints."

Clearly the "one baptism" means the baptism of the Spirit, as further demonstrated in 1 Corinthians 12:13—"For by one Spirit we were all baptized into one body—whether Jews or Greeks, whether slaves or free—and have all been made to drink into one Spirit." Water baptism, although not necessary for salvation, displays our identification with Jesus' death and resurrection. It simply becomes an outward act of association with Jesus, based upon the inward result of being baptized by the Spirit. In other words, water baptism doesn't save the soul. Paul demonstrated this when he wrote: "For Christ did not send me to baptize, but to preach the gospel" (1 Cor. 1:17). If submitting to water baptism could save the soul, Paul would have said, "For Christ sent me to baptize and to preach the gospel." When Paul delineated the essential features of the gospel message in 1 Corinthians 15:3–4, he didn't include baptism!

Finally, we have "One God and Father of all, who is above all, and through all, and in you all" (Eph. 4:6). Since the one baptism is Spirit baptism, then the moment someone is born again they are placed into the family of God. As a result, Galatians 4:6 offers, "And because you are sons, God has sent forth the Spirit of His Son into your hearts, crying out, Abba, Father." Observe also that Galatians 4:6 mentions all the members of the Trinity: Father, Son, and Holy Spirit. Knowing the need for unity within the body of Christ as modeled by the Trinity, none of us should be lining up in the Christian unemployment office!

PRACTICING THE ONENESS WALK—E

Our employment begins with this basic injunction: *Live in oneness by honoring your heavenly calling.* Consider a tuning fork. It delivers a true pitch by two tines vibrating together. Muffle either side, even a little, and the note disappears. Sounded individually neither tine can produce the sweet, pure note. Only when both tines vibrate is the correct pitch heard. God desires us, the body of Christ, to work in harmony to produce sweet, pure notes.

Satan exists to divide us, whereas Jesus exhorts us to have a spirit of unity. Once Jesus was accused of casting out demons by the power of Satan. His response, "Every kingdom divided against itself is brought to desolation, and every city or house divided against itself will not stand" (Matt. 12:25). From the beginning (see Genesis 3 and 4), Satan has connived to separate people from God and from one another. And Jesus came to undo the deeds of Satan: "For this purpose the Son of God was manifested, that He might destroy [or loose] the works of the devil" (1 John 3:8).

Eagerly pursue oneness in your marriage, home, and church while valuing your heavenly calling, leading a life of humility, and seeking to place Christ first and others ahead of yourself. A gentle, longsuffering spirit, coupled with the extra ingredient of bearing with one another in love, will produce a recipe of peace and harmony. Oneness begins with a godly mindset.

Ephesians 4:4–6 gives us the second employment point: *Live in oneness, like the Trinity.* The word "one" appears so many times in Ephesians 4:4–6 to drive home the message of unity for believers. God the Father, God the Son, and God the Holy Spirit are three persons with one essence. As the triune God functions with perfect union, so should the saints.

The heart of God took two separate, formerly hostile, ethnicities (Jew and Gentile) and formed one body called the church. Today as nations fight against nations, and people groups war against other people groups, and husbands and wives bicker, and families display dysfunctional tendencies, isn't it time for the church of Jesus Christ to do a better job of exhibiting the oneness of the Trinity?

How does God view unity among the saints? I leave you with the beautiful visual aids that Psalm 133 provides:

Behold, how good and how pleasant it is for brethren to dwell together in unity! It is like the precious oil upon the head, running down on the beard, the beard of Aaron, running down on the edge of his garments. It is like the dew of Hermon, descending upon the mountains of Zion; for there the Lord commanded the blessing—life forevermore.

CHAPTER ELEVEN

WHAT'S THE PURPOSE FOR BIBLICAL FOLLOW-THE-LEADER?

EPHESIANS 4:7–16

⌁⌁⌁

After hundreds of years the perfect pastor has been found! He is a church leader who will please everyone! He preaches exactly twenty minutes and then sits down. He condemns sin but never steps on anybody's toes. He makes $500 a week and gives $100 of that back to the church. He drives a late-model car, buys lots of books, wears fine clothes and has a very nice family. He's thirty-six years old and has been preaching for forty years. He's tall on the short side and heavyset in a thin sort of way. His eyes are either blue or brown, to fit the occasion. And he wears his hair parted in the middle; the left side is straight and the right side is wavy. He has a burning desire to work with the youth and spends all of his time with the senior citizens. He smiles all the time while keeping a straight face because he has a keen sense of humor, and this keeps him seriously dedicated. He makes fifteen calls a day on church members, spends all of his time evangelizing non-members, and is always found in his office studying when he's needed. Unfortunately he burned himself out and died at the age of thirty-two!

We are about to study Ephesians 4:7–16. Here we will not learn about the perfect pastor, but the pastor who perfects others:

> But to each one of us grace was given according to the measure of Christ's gift. Therefore He says: "When He ascended on high, He led captivity captive, And gave gifts to men." (Now this, "He ascended"—what does it mean but that he also first descended into the lower parts of the earth? He who descended is also the One who ascended far above all the heavens, that He might fill all

things.) And He Himself gave some to be apostles, some prophets, some evangelists, and some pastors and teachers, for the equipping of the saints for the work of ministry, for the edifying of the body of Christ, till we all come to the unity of the faith and the knowledge of the Son of God, to a perfect man, to the measure of the stature of the fullness of Christ; that we should no longer be children tossed to and fro and carried about with every wind of doctrine, by the trickery of men, in the cunning craftiness by which they lie in wait to deceive, but, speaking the truth in love, may grow up in all things into Him who is the head—Christ—from whom the whole body, joined and knit together by what every joint supplies, according to the effective working by which every part does its share, causes growth of the body for the edifying of itself in love.

EPHESIANS 4:7–16, NKJV

But to each one of us grace was given according to the measure of Christ's gift. Therefore it says, "When He ascended on high, He led captive a host of captives, and He gave gifts to men." (Now this expression, "He ascended," what does it mean except that He also had descended into the lower parts of the earth? He who descended is Himself also He who ascended far above all the heavens, so that He might fill all things.) And He gave some as apostles, and some as prophets, and some as evangelists, and some as pastors and teachers, for the equipping of the saints for the work of service, to the building up of the body of Christ; until we all attain to the unity of the faith, and of the knowledge of the Son of God, to a mature man, to the measure of the stature which belongs to the fullness of Christ. As a result, we are no longer to be children, tossed here and there by waves and carried about by every wind of doctrine, by the trickery of men, by craftiness in deceitful scheming; but speaking the truth in love, we are to grow up in all aspects into Him who is the head, even Christ, from whom the whole body, being fitted and held together by what every joint supplies, according to the proper working of each individual part, causes the growth of the body for the building up of itself in love.

EPHESIANS 4:7–16, NASB

PRACTICING THE ONENESS WALK—F

To become more familiar with the details of these verses, ask yourself the following questions:

- What does it mean, "But to each one of us grace was given" (v. 7)?
- What is "Christ's gift" (v. 7)?
- What does Paul refer to when he says in verse 7 that Jesus "first descended into the lower parts of the earth?"
- How do the gifted men given to the church relate to the concept of unity that we studied in Ephesians 4:1–6?
- Why does Paul use the word "for" three times in verse 12?
- How important is it that the sheep follow their leaders, according to verses 13–16?

PRACTICING THE ONENESS WALK—I

God has favored every saint with at least one spiritual gift. A spiritual gift differs from a talent. You were graced with certain abilities at your birth; these talents accompanied you from the moment of your arrival. A spiritual gift is a supernatural ability given by God (the Father, the Son, and the Holy Spirit) to believers at the moment of their salvation, for the purpose of building up the body of Christ: "But to each one of us grace was given according to the measure of Christ's gift" (Eph. 4:7). Upon your birth into the family of God, our benevolent Lord imparted to you a divine ability to labor for the Father, which involves serving your brothers and sisters in Christ.

"Christ's gift," came to us as a result of his victorious conquest. Paul cited Psalm 68:18 within Ephesians 4:8 to illustrate that our spoils came from our military hero. "Therefore He [Jesus] says, 'When He ascended on high, He led captivity captive, and gave gifts to men.'" Psalm 68 depicts a triumphant conqueror with prisoners, distributing gifts to the liberated people. In Ephesians 4:8, the champion becomes Christ dispensing gifts.

What foes did Jesus defeat? He subdued three enemies: sin, death, and Satan. Furthermore, he saved us, the former captives of Satan, and placed us in his service. Our Commander-in-Chief did more than rescue us from the clutches of the wicked Devil; He also doled out "gifts to men."

How did Jesus accomplish this? " He ascended"—what does it mean but that he also first descended into the lower parts of the earth?" (Eph. 4:9). Before Jesus could go up to heaven ("ascend"), he first had to come down to the earth. He accomplished this miracle through the virgin birth. Before Jesus could mount up to heaven—and impart the gifts to the church—He first came down by becoming a man (the Incarnation).

Is that what is meant by "the lower parts of the earth"? Although many have interpreted this to refer to Jesus' descent into hades after he died, this phrase isn't that complex. "Into the lower parts" most likely grammatically fits the category of a genitive of apposition (i.e., the word refers to the same thing as the word it modifies). Placed beside "the earth," it could mean the same thing; "the lower parts" could be just another description of "the earth." Either way, the writer wants to make clear that prior to rising to the right hand of God and sitting down, Jesus first had to come down to earth.

Jesus came to earth and won the victory over sin, death, and Satan. Subsequently, he returned to the Father "that He might fill all things" (Eph. 4:10). His return to the highest heavens—heaven itself—proves his right to rule over the universe and dispense the gifts cited in the next verse.

Jesus is heaven's distributor. He determines the needs of each church and then fills the order. Ephesians 4:11 testifies, "And He Himself gave some to be apostles, some prophets, some evangelists, and some pastors and teachers." Gifts have been given to these leaders, and they are Christ's gift to the church.

Evangelists, for example, carry the good news to the unsaved. Although they function outside the church winning the lost, they also serve inside the body of Christ by training others to do the work of evangelists. Their God-given ability equips them to be on the forefront of evangelism both locally and globally.

The expression "pastors and teachers" is governed by one article (the word "the") in the Greek. It shows one office with two functions. Biblically speaking, not all teachers are pastors but all pastors should be teachers. The primary function of the pastor consists of feeding the sheep.

Observe the three uses of "for" in Ephesians 4:12. The apostles, prophets, evangelists, and pastors/teachers exist, "for the equipping of the saints for the work of ministry, for the edifying of the body of Christ." The noun "equipping" means *to make completely prepared*. Evangelists and pastors/teachers train believers not only to effectively serve in the church but also "for the edifying of the body of Christ." These spiritual personal trainers have a vital role to build up the spiritual muscles of those in the church.

Maturity in the church (which produces unity) becomes the goal for spiritual leaders. Paul's objective is clear, "Till we all come to the unity of the faith and the knowledge of the Son of God, to a perfect man, to the measure of the stature of the fullness of Christ" (Eph. 4:13). Good shepherds want the entire flock—notice the word "all"—to exhibit oneness by obtaining a full knowledge of Jesus. The result of pastoral training should produce a full-grown flock of sheep that, when evaluated, matches up with their spiritual head, Jesus.

Stability that comes from maturity will ensure "...that we should no longer be children, tossed to and fro and carried about with every wind of doctrine, by the trickery of men, in the cunning craftiness by which they lie in wait to deceive" (Eph. 4:14). "Children" derives from a compound Greek word and means *not able to speak*. Paul didn't want the Ephesians to end up like immature children who are too young to speak.

Satan delights to prey upon undeveloped saints, and one of his goals for believers is immaturity. He wants them to be "tossed to and fro with every wind of doctrine." Bad doctrine propagated by the "trickery of men" is designed to keep God's children off-balance spiritually. The word "trickery" comes from the root *dice* and implies cheating, and this is facilitated by men's "cunning craftiness." (The NASB translation says this is accomplished "by craftiness in deceitful scheming." Literally this could be translated as "toward the method of deception.") The wicked one has mastered the timeless methods that can cause God's children to wander from the truth.

How does our heavenly Father recommend that we counter the Serpent's manifold manipulations? Paul offers, "But, speaking the truth in love...grow up in all things into Him who is the head—Christ" (Eph. 4:15). The truth of God's Word will keep the saints biblically balanced so that they won't embark on a slipshod course of doctrinal destruction.

A mature fellowship of believers under the direction of Jesus will produce coming-of-age saints who exhibit a spirit of unity. Then, "the whole body, joined and knit together by what every joint supplies, according to the effective working by which every part does it share, causes growth of the body for the edifying of itself in love" (Eph. 4:16).

PRACTICING THE ONENESS WALK—R

Paul began our section of Scripture pointing out that every believer has received at least one spiritual gift: "But to each one of us grace was given according to the measure of Christ's gift" (Eph. 4:7). 1 Peter 4:10 concurs: "As each one has received a gift, minister it to one another, as good stewards of the manifold grace of God." Peter's choice of Greek word for "gift" literally means *the result of grace*. Both Paul and Peter portray the purpose of these grace gifts as for the betterment of Christ's body.

No child of God has the right to boast about his or her giftedness; it is the byproduct of God's favor. The Corinthians lacked "no gift," according to 1 Corinthians 1:7. Yet instead of being humbled by God's grace, they became haughty. Paul reminded them in 1 Corinthians 4:7, "And what do you have that you did not receive? Now if you did indeed receive it, why do you glory as if you had not received it?" Paul shows that even the choosing of the gift depends upon divinely sovereign, not human, choice: "But one and the same Spirit works all these things, distributing to each one individually as He wills" (1 Cor. 12:11).

Paul points to Jesus as the allocator of spiritual gifts (Eph. 4:7). Peter attributes them to "the manifold grace of God" (1 Pet. 4:10). And the Spirit imparts them as he providentially chooses (1 Cor. 12:11). Thus we see that a spiritual gift is a supernatural ability given by God (in Trinity) to believers at the moment of salvation for the building up of the body of Christ.

On a practical note, you may be asking, "What is my spiritual gift?" Thirty-five years of church ministry has taught me that the best place to discover your gift is in your local church. Ask God to guide you to the realm of service that will best glorify him. When you find the role that brings you the greatest amount of ministry satisfaction, this becomes one confirmation that you've found your gift. Also, others will encourage you that they have been blessed by your service. That is another confirmation. For me, God drew me toward teaching, which cut across my natural grain, and then used seasoned saints to confirm my gift of teaching.

One of the gifts given to the church is evangelism. The word "evangelist" occurs three times in the Greek New Testament. Besides Ephesians 4:11, it appears in Acts 21:8 where Luke (the author of Acts) calls Philip "the evangelist." Philip was one of seven men who had been chosen (Acts 6) to help meet the needs of the widows. After that we find him (Acts 8) carrying out the function of an evangelist.

Philip shouldered Jesus' assignment (as given in Acts 1:8) by preaching to those who lived in Samaria (Acts 8:5). He had a successful ministry where many had come to Christ (Acts 8:6). Next, the Spirit of God dispatched him to the remote Philistine city of Gaza, where he found an Ethiopian eunuch whom he led to Christ. Once he finished that assignment, God moved him on to another Philistine city, Azotus, from which he continued to preach in all the cities along the way to Caesarea. Clearly Philip fulfilled his calling as a traveling evangelist.

The third use of "evangelist" arises in 2 Timothy 4:5, referring to Timothy, who may or may not have had the gift of evangelism. Either way, Paul told him, "But you be watchful in all things, endure afflictions, do the work of an evangelist, fulfill your ministry." I personally lean toward the view that Timothy didn't possess the evangelistic gift; his personality seems to lean toward shyness (2 Tim. 1:7), which doesn't fit the typical evangelists I know. However, while he remained at Ephesus, Paul expected him to accomplish that assignment. This shows us that although not all of us have the specific gift of evangelism, we are all commanded to be witnesses for Jesus.

Let's move on to the pastor/teacher gifts. The word "pastor" means *shepherd.* John 10 describes the shepherd as the protector of the flock. Hanging on the wall in my study is a picture that I took in 1993 while in Bethlehem. The snapshot captures a shepherd leading his sheep, and this has become a picture of what I want to model to my flock: "And when he [the good shepherd] brings out his own sheep, he goes before them; and the sheep follow him, for they know his voice" (John 10:4). Middle Eastern shepherds do not drive their sheep; they lead them. Similarly, pastors should be out in front of their congregations, portraying a Christlike life that is worth following.

Finally, but certainly not insignificantly, the shepherd must feed the sheep. As you are aware, Peter denied the Lord three times before his crucifixion. After his resurrection, Jesus appeared to Peter to restore him privately (Luke 24:34; 1 Cor. 15:5), but since Peter had denied Jesus publicly, he needed to be held accountable before his fellow disciples and to be restored in their midst. John records Peter's public restoration. Jesus asked Peter, "Do you love Me more than these?" (John 21:15). He was referring to Peter's boast that although the other disciples might deny him, he wouldn't. As Jesus probed the once-proud disciple, he also exhorted him toward pastoral service. He commanded, "Feed My lambs" (v. 15), "Tend My sheep," (v. 16), and "Feed My sheep" (v. 17). The Master Teacher drove home the point that feeding the sheep via preaching and teaching are essential components of a shepherd's ministry.

God gives gifted men to the church to perfect the saints. Sheep often come with problems that need to be fixed. Another way to put it is that they have holes that need to be plugged. A verbal form of the word for "equipping" (Eph. 4:12) occurs in Matthew 4:21, where it is translated "mending," with reference to James and John, with their father Zebedee, repairing their fishing nets. A net with a gaping hole in it will not catch fish. Similarly, a saint whose life needs patching must sit under the teaching ministry of a gifted pastor in order to be whole enough to do the work of ministry.

Another passage using the verb for "equipping" appears in Galatians 6:1, where Paul exhorted the mature saints—which most certainly would include the pastors—to do a spiritual intervention on behalf of hurting sheep and to make them whole. "Brethren, if a man is overtaken in any trespass, you who are spiritual restore such a one in a spirit of gentleness, considering yourself lest you also be tempted." The word "restore" is related to both "equipping" (Eph. 4:12) and "mending" (Matt. 4:21). Interestingly, in secular language this Greek word was used for setting broken bones. In the same way that a physician would gently treat a patient with a broken bone, well-seasoned leaders need to graciously "restore" sheep that have taken a spiritual tumble!

The Lord Jesus cares greatly for the sheep. He has demonstrated this through entrusting evangelists, pastors, and teachers to equip the saints to do the work of the Lord.

PRACTICING THE ONENESS WALK—E

I have often heard it said that doctrine divides. Would God give gifted teachers to the church to be fractious? No! Good doctrine, when heeded, doesn't divide but instead creates a united church. Remember that our chapter began with Paul's appeal to the saints for unity (Eph. 4:3), and that the model was derived from the Trinity. Keep this in mind as you contemplate your first employment point: *Jesus gives gifts for the sake of a united church* (Eph. 4:7–11).

What does God expect us to do when we've received a gift? After all, James 1:17 informs us, "Every good gift and every perfect gift is from above, and comes down from the Father of lights, with whom there is no variation or shadow of turning." Knowing that evangelism, shepherding, and teaching are God' gifts to the church, take some time right now and thank him for those presents. In particular, express your appreciation to the Father for the evangelists and pastors/teachers in your life. Next, write a note of encouragement to the evangelists, pastors/teachers in your church. Let them know that you've been studying Ephesians 4 and want them to be aware just how grateful you are for them. I've heard it said that ministry that costs nothing is worth nothing. There are many ways to show your support, such as giving them a gift card or a love gift toward a family getaway, or whatever you think would be a blessing to them.

Our second application point is, *Follow Jesus' gifted leaders for unity and maturity* (Eph. 4:12–16). There exists a danger when sheep follow other sheep and not the shepherds that God has provided. I came upon the following illustration from *Preaching Today* that illustrates this well:

> It all started with one self-destructive leap.
>
> Shepherds eating breakfast outside the town of Gevas, Turkey were surprised to see a lone sheep jump off of a nearby cliff and fall to its death. They were stunned, however, when the rest of the nearly 1,500 sheep in the herd followed, each leaping off the same cliff.
>
> When it was all over, the local Aksam newspaper reported that "450 of the sheep perished in a billowy, white pile" (those that jumped from the middle and end of the herd were saved as the pile became higher and the fall more cushioned). The estimated loss to the families of Gevas tops $100,000, an extremely significant amount of money in a country where the average person earns about $2,700 annually.
>
> "There's nothing we can do. They're all wasted," said Nevzat Bayhan, a member of one of the 26 families whose sheep were grazing together in the herd.[1]

The above example shows why sheep should follow their shepherd and not other sheep. Submission to walk behind your church leaders is a deliberate choice. We must bow our heads and hearts to God and tell Him that we will, by the grace of God, stay close on the heels of those God has placed over us. As I suggested above, you can also share with your pastor a note of encouragement and support, which I can tell you from experience will be immensely appreciated.

CHAPTER TWELVE

WHEN IS IT ALL RIGHT TO PUT SOMEONE OFF?

EPHESIANS 4:17–24

〰〰

After a minister had preached a searching sermon on pride, a woman who had heard the sermon waited to talk to the preacher. She seemed distressed and told the preacher she needed to confess a great sin. The minister asked, "What is this great sin?"

She replied, "Pride, for every day I spend an hour before the mirror adoring my beauty."

The pastor, after taking a long look at her, answered, "You don't have the sin of pride; you have the sin of imagination!"

In 1895, William R. Newell penned the words to the well-known hymn, "At Calvary." The first stanza goes, "Years I spent in vanity and pride, caring not my Lord was crucified, knowing not it was for me He died at Calvary." These words capture the essence of the Ephesians' "imagination" prior to coming to Christ.

In Ephesians 4:17–24, Paul exhorted them concerning what they, as children of God, needed to "put off," and then what they needed to "put on":

> This I say, therefore, and testify in the Lord, that you should no longer walk as the rest of the Gentiles walk, in the futility of their mind, having their understanding darkened, being alienated from the life of God, because of the ignorance that is in them, because of the hardening of their heart; who, being past feeling, have given themselves over to licentiousness, to work all uncleanness with greediness. But you have not so learned Christ, if indeed you have

heard Him and have been taught by Him, as the truth is in Jesus: that you put off, concerning your former conduct, the old man which grows corrupt according to the deceitful lusts, and be renewed in the spirit of your mind, and that you put on the new man which was created according to God, in righteousness and true holiness.

EPHESIANS 4:17–24, NKJV

So I say this, and insist in the Lord, that you no longer live as the Gentiles do, in the futility of their thinking. They are darkened in their understanding, being alienated from the life of God because of the ignorance that is in them due to the hardness of their hearts. Because they are callous, they have given themselves over to indecency for the practice of every kind of impurity with greediness. But you did not learn about Christ like this, if indeed you heard about him and were taught in him, just as the truth is in Jesus. You were taught with reference to your former way of life to lay aside the old man who is being corrupted in accordance with deceitful desires, to be renewed in the spirit of your mind, and to put on the new man who has been created in God's image—in righteousness and holiness that comes from truth.

EPHESIANS 4:17–24, NET

SOMETHING OLD AND SOMETHING NEW—F

Our questions for these verses will help us dig more deeply into God's Word:

- What is the "therefore" there for (Eph. 4:17)?
- What does the expression, "in the futility of their mind" mean (Eph. 4:17)?
- What caused the Ephesians to have "their understanding darkened" (Eph. 4:18)?
- What does "being past feeling" mean (Eph. 4:19)?
- Why does Ephesians 4:20 read, "But you have not so learned

Christ" and not, "But you have not so learned *about* Christ?"
- How are you supposed to be "renewed in the spirit of your mind" (Eph. 4:23)?

SOMETHING OLD AND SOMETHING NEW—I

Did you grow up on "schoolhouse rock"? I did. Although I don't remember much from those lessons, I do recall the statement, "Conjunction junction, what's your function?" Paul used the inferential conjunction "therefore" in verse 17 when he wrote, "This I say, therefore." The word serves as the junction between God's gifted men who were to train the Ephesians for maturity (4:7–16) with what he was about to write (Eph. 4:17–29).

Since the Ephesians had gifted men to train them to do the work of ministry and to promote their spiritual growth, Paul told them, "...no longer walk as the rest of the Gentiles walk, in the futility of their mind." "The rest of the Gentiles" refers to non-Jewish pagans, and these born-again believers were admonished not to imitate them "in the futility of their mind." "Futility" means *vanity* or *worthlessness*. Paul insisted that they shouldn't live like the purposeless heathen in their thoughts or actions.

The unsaved are further described as "having their understanding darkened, being alienated from the life of God because of the ignorance that is in them" (Eph. 4:18). Why would these saints, whose minds had once been unable to see the light of God, and who had been separated from the Lord because of their lack of biblical knowledge and their hearts of stone, want to regress to that previous lifestyle?

Paul continued, "...who, being past feeling, have given themselves over to licentiousness, to work all uncleanness with greediness" (Eph. 4:19). The two English words "past feeling" (one word in the Greek) have a fascinating meaning. The word has an alpha privative, which is equivalent to the way we add the letter "a" to certain words in order to negate the meaning of that term. For instance, "amoral" means *not having a moral sense*. In this case, the root word of "past feeling" gives us the English word "analgesic" which means *feeling no pain*. Paul is describing the lost as having no moral compass, as feeling no embarrassment or shame on account of their sin.

Metaphorically, prior to salvation the Ephesians had been on an "unsaved aspirin" regimen that deadened their conscience. Unsaved people are described as having "given themselves over to licentiousness," which speaks of sexual excess, a total lack of restraint. The unsavory heathen lifestyle embraces "all uncleanness with greediness," and is characterized by self-indulgent perversion.

"But you have not so learned Christ" (Eph. 4:20), countered Paul. He pointed to the Ephesians and said, "you [emphatic in the Greek] know Jesus differently." It intrigues me that Paul omitted the word "about." He didn't say, "But you have not so learned *about* Christ." Why? Because Christianity, unlike all religions that preach a works-based salvation, begins and ends with a personal relationship with Jesus Christ. (As I was composing this chapter, Billy Graham was in the news since it was his ninety-fifth birthday. You can read books about Billy Graham, but that is vastly different than knowing him personally.) These believers knew Jesus experientially—and just knowing Jesus means that you walk away from the lusts of this world.

Every word-choice carries significant meaning in the Greek. In verse 21, Paul used a first-class condition, writing, "...if indeed you have heard Him and have been taught by Him, as the truth is in Jesus." A first class condition means you assume the "if" to be true. The implication is, "...*since* indeed you have heard Him and have been taught by Him, as the truth is in Jesus." Jesus, by the Spirit and the written Word of God, has instructed all saints so that they know his truth.

In verses 22 through 24, the apostle to the Gentiles gave the Ephesians guidance that should apply to all believers: "...that you put off, concerning your former conduct, the old man which grows corrupt according to the deceitful lusts" (Eph. 4:22). Since these saints have been placed spiritually in heavenly realms with Christ, and have been instructed for maturity, they should refrain from allowing their inherited fallen nature from Adam to seduce them any longer.

How can this be possible? These old passions are strong. Verse 23 to the rescue: "...and be renewed in the spirit of your mind." "Renewed," of course, means, "again new." The verb's voice is passive, which means that you need to allow something in order to be made new. We will further examine what produces this newness in the next section.

Finally, once something is "put off," then something new can be "put on": "...put on the new man which was created according to God, in righteousness and true holiness" (Eph. 4:24). Here, the word "new" differs from the word "new" used in the compound Greek word, "renewed" in the previous verse. In v. 23 the word "new" means *new in relation to time* or *that which has recently come into* existence, whereas in verse 24 it means *new in the aspect of quality* because God has given you *a new kind of life.* You received a new capacity the moment you were born again. We will revisit this distinction in the next section.

SOMETHING OLD AND SOMETHING NEW—R

Paul reported in Ephesians 4:18 about the lost "having their understanding darkened." The tense of the word "darkened" in Greek makes it clear that the unsaved have been in the dark in the past, with the results of that blindness continuing. Moreover, the voice of the passive verb shows that an outside influence has contributed to their condition.

What caused the darkness? In Romans 1:18–3:20, Paul, in one fell swoop, bundled all of mankind into a single package labeled "sinners." He depicted the degeneration of humankind, from knowing the Father God in the beginning (Adam and Eve) to preferring the father of lies (Satan): "...because, although they knew God, they did not glorify Him as God, nor were thankful, but became futile in their thoughts, and their foolish hearts were darkened" (Rom. 1:21).

Satan, the prince of darkness, contributes to the world's plight of blindness: "But even if our gospel is veiled, it is veiled to those who are perishing" wrote Paul to the Corinthians, "whose minds the god of this age has blinded, who do not believe, lest the light of the gospel of the glory of Christ, who is the image of God, should shine on them" (2 Cor. 4:3–4).

Why have the people of the world become corrupted or, as Paul laments, "past feeling," having "given themselves over to licentiousness, to work all uncleanness with greediness" (Eph. 4:19)? As we saw earlier from Romans 1, people knew God, but rejected Him. Rom. 1:25 adds, "...who exchanged the truth of God for the lie, and worshipped and served the creature rather than the Creator, who is blessed forever." Since people rejected God, He turned them over to their own futile imaginations. On account of this, three times Paul stated that "God gave them up" or "God gave them over" to their own devices (see Romans 1:24, 26, 28).

Paul, true to his shepherd's heart, then exhorted the Ephesians concerning what to "put off" and what to "put on," as well as their need to "be renewed in the spirit of your mind" (Eph. 4:23). This idea (which implies that when Jesus died on the cross, so did we) also connects with the larger body of Scripture. Galatians 2:20 testifies to this biblical truth: "I have been crucified with Christ." Romans 6:6 builds upon it: "Knowing this, that our old man was crucified with Him, that the body of sin might be done away with [rendered inoperative or nullified], that we should no longer be slaves of sin." Think about it—dead people don't give in to temptation!

We've not only been co-crucified with Christ, but also co-resurrected with Him: "If [another first class condition, assumed to be true] then you were raised with Christ, seek those things which are above, where Christ is, sitting at the right hand of God. Set your mind on things above, not on the things on the earth. For you died, and your life is hidden with Christ in God" (Col. 3:1–3). Paul presented the "put on" and "put off" theme often: "But now you must also put off all these.... Do not lie to one another, since you have put off the old man with his deeds, and have put on the new man who is renewed in knowledge according to the image of Him who created Him" (Col. 3:8–10).

The new man arrived upon our belief in Jesus' death and resurrection: "Therefore, if anyone is in Christ, he is a new creation; old things have passed away; behold, all things have become new" (2 Cor. 5:17). However, the child of God must commit "to be renewed in the spirit of [his or her] mind" (Eph. 4:23). I recently looked into an old Bible that I had used when I first became a Christian, and next to the reference Ephesians 4:23, I had marked, May 19, 1980. I must have been studying this passage or listening to a sermon, approximately three years after I was saved, and I made a commitment to apply this verse personally. In other words, I determined to *employ* the truth, just as we are about to do in the next section.

SOMETHING OLD AND SOMETHING NEW—E

Our first employment point tells us what to do: *Put off the heathen in you* (Eph. 4:17–22). Adam is alive and well in each of us; his fallen nature has been passed down to you and me. Therefore we need to practice our heavenly placement, and keep the old man crucified.

I don't find it a coincidence that Paul put verse 23 ("And be renewed in the spirit of your mind") between verse 22, in which he exhorted the Ephesians to "put off" the old, and verse 24, in which he exhorted them to "put on" the new. God's Word, housed deeply in our hearts and minds, gives us the leverage to practice our position.

Practically speaking, how does this work? The psalmist poses it as a question: "How can a young man cleanse his way?" (Ps. 119:9a). The psalmist then answers his own question. "By taking heed according to Your word. With my whole heart I have sought You; oh, let me not wander from Your commandments! Your word I have hidden in my heart, that I might not sin against You" (Ps. 119:9b–11).

Put off the heathen in you, starting with an awareness of your position in Christ because of the power of the cross: Because you have been co-crucified with Jesus on the cross, you don't need to respond to the beckoning of the old sin nature any longer. We need to digest Romans 6:1–2, which reads, "What shall we say then? Shall we continue in sin that grace may abound? Certainly not! How shall we who died to sin live any longer in it?" Close your eyes for a moment and envision yourself on the cross with Jesus. Death means separation from the previous life. Don't resurrect your old man; let him stay co-crucified with Jesus.

Scripture memorization is a powerful tool, and in conjunction with this first employment, I want you to memorize Galatians 2:20. "I have been crucified with Christ; it is no longer I who live, but Christ lives in me; and the life which I now live in the flesh I live by faith in the Son of God, who loved me and gave Himself for me." *Put off the heathen in you* by hiding this Word in your heart.

Our second employment point is the "put on" part (Eph. 4:23–24): *Put on the heaven in you.* The doctrinal foundation for this divine enablement arose from Ephesians 1:1–3:21. This is why Paul could say, "And be renewed in the spirit of your mind, and…put on the new man which was created according to God, in righteousness and true holiness" (Eph. 4:23–24).

Not only picture yourself as co-crucified with Jesus, but imagine yourself as resurrected with Him. I highly recommend a dedicated regimen of Scripture memorization. You won't always have your Bible when the Devil comes calling, so prudently prepare by memorizing Scripture so that you can recall it from your mind at any moment. *Put on the heaven in you* by storing up (memorizing) profound truths such as this one from Paul's letter to the Colossians:

> If then you were raised with Christ, seek those things which are above, where Christ is, sitting at the right hand of God. Set your mind on things above, not on things on the earth. For you died, and your life is hidden with Christ in God. When Christ who *is* our life appears, then you also will appear with Him in glory.

> COLOSSIANS 3:1–4

CHAPTER THIRTEEN

FOUR COMMON PRACTICES OF OUR OLD NATURE

EPHESIANS 4:25–29

⟡

The witty Mark Twain once wrote, "A lie can travel halfway around the world while the truth is putting on its shoes." The old nature can produce some uncouth habits, such as lying, that need to be put to death permanently. Paul addressed four of them in particular in Ephesians 4:25–29. Meditatively read over the following verses that address the remedy pertaining to four common practices of our unredeemed human nature:

> Therefore, putting away lying, each one speak truth with his neighbor, for we are members of one another. "Be angry, and do not sin": do not let the sun go down on your wrath, nor give place to the devil. Let him who stole steal no longer, but rather let him labor, working with his hands what is good, that he may have something to give him who has need. Let no corrupt communication proceed out of your mouth, but what is good for necessary edification, that it may impart grace to the hearers.
>
> EPHESIANS 4:25–29, NKJV

> We are part of the same body. Stop lying and start telling each other the truth. Don't get so angry that you sin. Don't go to bed angry and don't give the devil a chance. If you are a thief, quit stealing. Be honest and work hard, so you will have something to give to people in need. Stop all your dirty talk. Say the right thing at the right time and help others by what you say.
>
> EPHESIANS 4:25–29, CEV

THE PRACTICES OF THE NEW MAN—F

- What is the "therefore" there for (v. 25)?
- What exactly is a lie?
- Why would Paul write to "be angry" (v. 26)?
- What is the connection between "not letting the sun go down upon your wrath," and "giving place to the devil" (vv. 26–27)?
- What are some ways that people steal today, and how should that activity be replaced according to verse 28?
- What does the word "corrupt," mean (v. 29)?

THE PRACTICES OF THE NEW MAN—I

The "therefore" in verse 25 strategically links the idea of "putting off" former conduct (v. 22) with the four common practices that follow (verses 25–29).

Paul placed "lying" at the head of the list. A lie contradicts facts, with the purpose of manipulation or deception. To put away lying literally means, "to lay down lying."

For example, if I tell you that you can view my sermons at colmarmanorbible.ord, and I meant to say colmarmanorbible.org, I didn't lie because the intent wasn't deception. However, if I tell you the wrong website address deliberately because I don't want you to watch my sermons, then I would have concocted a lie. Instead of lying, the apostle commanded, "Each one speak truth with his neighbor for we are members of one another." The members of the body of Christ have the mandate to communicate with honesty and integrity within the ranks since we belong to each other.

After telling them to set aside falsehoods, Paul gave a second command: "Be angry, and do not sin" (v. 26). The word for "anger" appears eight times in the Greek New Testament, and none of the seven other references give this positive kind of command. Although righteous anger over unjust deeds can be warranted, we need to make sure we don't cross the line, lapsing into sin (see again v. 26). Even justified anger can quickly change into sinful anger.

An interesting nexus that crops up in verses 26b through 27, where

Paul warned the Ephesians, "Do not let the sun go down upon your wrath, nor give place to the devil." Unchecked anger opens up a door for Satan in your life. A lack of self-control can enable Satan to get a foothold in your life and home.

The third imperative comes up in Ephesians 4:28—"Let him who stole steal no longer, but rather let him labor, working with his hands what is good, that he may have something to give him who has need." The apostle's advice to former thieves: Learn to *labor to the point of exhaustion* (which is the meaning of "labor") and benefit others by sharing your earnings with those who have need.

Finally, Paul commands: "Let no corrupt communication proceed out of your mouth, but what is good for necessary edification, that it may impart grace to the hearers" (v. 29). "Corrupt" arises eight times in the Greek New Testament, and six of the eight instances deal with bad or rotten fruit. When we speak out of our old nature, it's as if we have putrid or rotten fruit spewing from our lips. This gross image portrays those times when people use the Lord's name in vain or curse or utter words not fitting for Christians.

So Paul wants Christians to bury (along with their old nature) ungodly behaviors such as lying, sinful anger, stealing, and "dirty talk" (see the CEV translation above). He then told the saints how the new man should talk by qualifying it with the following words, "...what is good for necessary edification." Literally, "edification" means *to build a house.* Our verbal communication should be upbuilding, always encouraging our brothers and sisters in Christ toward spiritual growth. The wise apostle added, "...that it may impart grace to the hearers." When Jesus implanted a new nature within you, He embedded in you the capacity to address others in a way that builds them up in his own supernatural grace.

THE PRACTICES OF THE NEW MAN—R

God cannot lie. The ninth commandment written by Moses reflects his truthful nature, "You shall not bear false witness against your neighbor" (Ex. 20:16). Jesus built upon this concept, praying to his Father: "Sanctify them [his disciples] by Your truth. Your word is truth" (John 17:17). Paul also understood the character of the Lord; therefore he wrote, "[put] away lying, [and] each one speak truth with his neighbor" (Eph. 4:25).

Untruth has its origin in the Devil. When Jesus spoke to a group of unsaved hostile Jews, he said about Satan, "He was a murderer from the beginning, and does not stand in the truth, because there is no truth in him. When he speaks a lie, he speaks from his own resources, for he is a liar and the father of it" (John 8:44). Those who don't repent of their lying ways and believe in Jesus will spend their eternity in hell, as described by the apostle John in the Book of Revelation: "But outside are dogs and sorcerers and sexually immoral and murderers and idolaters, and whoever loves and practices a lie" (Rev. 22:15).

If you want direct evidence of how important telling the truth is to the Lord, just look at the story of Ananias and Sapphira in the fourth chapter of the Book of Acts. Because of the poverty of many members of the early church in Jerusalem, the believers pooled their resources: "Nor was there anyone among them who lacked; for all who were possessors of lands or houses sold them, and brought the proceeds of the things that were sold, and laid them at the apostles' feet; and they distributed to each as anyone had need" (Acts 4:34–35). In particular, Barnabas sold some land and brought the earnings to the apostles (Acts 4:36–37), and his generosity was praised by the church.

Then along came Ananias and Sapphira. This Christian couple also sold their land, but unlike Barnabas, who had given all of his proceeds to the church leadership, they only pretended that they were doing the same. (Acts 5:1–11 records the story.) In order to receive glory, they attempted to deceive Peter and the others into thinking that they were giving all of the money, when in fact they were holding some back. Peter accused each one of them of lying not only to the church leaders, but primarily to the Holy Spirit (v. 3), whom he also called God (v. 4). They did not repent of their lie, and, without warning, both husband and wife were struck dead on the spot (Acts 5:5, 10).

Moving on to anger (Eph. 4:26), Paul quotes from Psalm 4:4, "Be angry, and do not sin." The Son of Man demonstrated what truly righteous anger looks like. One day he entered the temple, "And He found in the temple [precincts] those who sold oxen and sheep and doves, and the moneychangers doing business" (John 2:14). Although having animals and birds to purchase was an important feature of the sacrificial system, it seems that exorbitant rates were being charged, and Jesus was angry about it, because this activity displayed contempt for God's house: "When He had made a whip of cords, He drove them all out of the temple, with the sheep and the oxen, and poured out the changers' money and overturned the tables. And He said to those who sold doves, 'Take these things away! Do not make My Father's house a house of merchandise!'" (John 2:15–16). Jesus' display of appropriate anger also fulfilled an Old Testament Scripture, which John quotes in verse 17: "Zeal for Your house has eaten Me up" (from Psalm 69:9).

Needless to say, it's a fine line between righteous anger and sin. Moreover, inappropriate anger opens an avenue for Satan to encroach upon a believer's life. Jesus could model appropriate anger, but we need to take the cautionary words of Ephesians 4:26–27 to heart.

Before the days of Caller ID, I received a call from a man who wanted my pastoral blessing. What in particular did he want me to bless? The answer: He wanted me to give my consent to a murder he planned to commit. This man had been betrayed by someone, and he wanted a pastor to religiously sanction his act of revenge. Many thoughts raced through my mind, especially after this individual told me that he belonged to Mensa (an organization for the highly intelligent) and that he had the capacity to plan and execute this murder in such a way that he would never be suspected of the crime. Of course I knew that I had to confront him about his festering anger issue rather than endorsing the sin of murder. But based upon what I was about to do, I also wondered, "Does this man know where I live?"

He went on to share with me (in great detail) how he'd been mistreated. I could sympathize with his deep hurt but could never justify his retaliatory scheme. After listening to his grievance for about forty-five minutes, it was my turn to talk. He thanked me for my undivided attention. I took some time to point out that his antagonist had perpetrated a horrible act against him, but that to take his life was simply not justifiable. I wanted to share the gospel with this lost soul, but first I had to build the case that he was a sinner. I demonstrated the linkage that Jesus made in Matthew 5:21–22 between anger and murder. Furthermore, I pled the scriptural principle that the intent to murder was just as wrong as the act itself. This vengeful man listened with the utmost interest as I shared that Jesus came to take upon himself our sin (including anger), and that through belief in Jesus' substitutionary atonement and subsequent resurrection, we could be saved. I wish I could report that he repented and trusted Christ; however, I do believe that this man was greatly convicted of his sin and that he understood why he should not follow through on his unholy aspiration.

Let's now transition to the topic of stealing (v. 28), where Paul furnished the appropriate remediation for the crime: "Let him who stole steal no longer, but rather let him labor, working with his hands what is good, that he may have something to give him who has need." Those who have stolen in the past should now work not only to supply their personal or family needs, but also to help supply what others lack. When you set aside something bad (like stealing), you should replace it with something good (like meeting the needs of others).

This isn't the only place that the Bible recommends work as a blessing. God knew that a job would be beneficial for Adam, so he employed him in the Garden of Eden. The curse didn't come until after Adam and Eve disobeyed God (and even then, the ground received a curse, not the work). Paul shared with the saints at Galatia, "Therefore, as we have opportunity, let us do good to all, especially to those who are of the household of faith" (Gal. 6:10). I would even go so far as to say that when God provides a good job for you, that means it is the right *season* (the literal meaning of "opportunity") to begin to help furnish the needs of your brothers and sisters in Christ.

Paul added one final thing to "put off"—"Let no corrupt communication proceed out of your mouth, but what is good for necessary edification, that it may impart grace to the hearers" (Eph. 4:29). Bad speech patterns must be replaced with words that strengthen the lives of others. Colossians 4:6 tells us how to please God with our talk, "Let your speech always be with grace, seasoned with salt, that you may know how you ought to answer each one."

Once you are on the way to maturity, position meets practice.

THE PRACTICES OF THE NEW MAN—E

Ask yourself a difficult question. Although you may fully believe that lying, anger, stealing, and foul speech belong to your old nature, have you put these things aside entirely? Have you put on the new nature? A vital aspect of the Christian life involves putting on the new by employing the commands given by Paul in verses 25 through 29.

Paul tells us to put away lying (Eph. 4:25). *Practice your position by putting away lying* becomes our first employment point. We must set aside untruth and break the habit of "stretching" the truth. Not only that, but you and I must "speak truth with his neighbor for we are members of one another" (Eph. 4:25b). Let's put off the old lying ways that Satan has inspired, and put on the new speech pattern of truth that pleases God.

Your second employment point: *Practice your position by putting away anger* (Eph. 4:26–27). Don't assume that your anger is righteous; it is all too easy to allow it to move toward sinful anger. Remember that the final fruit of the Spirit given in Galatians 5:23 is "self-control." Even when Jesus drove the moneychangers out of the temple, he never lost his composure. Meditate on Scriptures that pertain to anger; this can become a key strategy for overcoming this potentially deadly habit. For example, here are two proverbs that might help you defeat anger: "He who is slow to anger is better than the mighty, and he who rules his spirit than he who takes a city" (Prov. 16:32). Indeed, "The discretion of a man makes him slow to anger, And it is to his glory to overlook a transgression" (Prov. 19:11).

As you allow God's powerful Word to take root in your heart, you will experience victory over both lying and anger. Simultaneously turn your attention to application point number three: *Practice your position by putting away stealing* (Eph. 4:28). Simply stated, don't help yourself to anything that doesn't belong to you.

Stealing doesn't just refer to taking someone else's property. We can steal by failing to work to earn our pay from an employer. Paul modeled how Christians must conduct themselves in the workplace: "For you yourselves know how you ought to follow us, for we were not disorderly among you; nor did we eat anyone's bread free of charge, but worked with labor and toil night and day, that we might not be a burden to any of you" (2 Thess. 3:7–8).

Finally, *practice your new position by putting away corrupt speech* (Eph. 4:29). Our fourth employment point commissions us not to be a "sewer spewer" when it comes to speech. Remember the adage concerning computers: "garbage in; garbage out." We need to guard our minds diligently and not take in the garbage that pours our through television, movies, radio, and DVDs so that we don't find ourselves pouring garbage out through our speech.

We are supposed to be like Jesus. What flowed from his lips? After he taught in the synagogue, Luke recorded: "So all bore witness to Him, and marveled at the gracious words which proceeded out of His mouth" (Luke 4:29). May God help all of us to represent our Lord well by putting away lying, anger, stealing, and corrupt speech.

CHAPTER FOURTEEN

WHEN YOU HAVE NO PAIN AND NO GAIN

EPHESIANS 4:30–32

A vehicle has a lot of working parts. When any one of those strategically assembled pieces malfunctions, we can find ourselves stranded. With modern cars come dashboard warning lights, or as a mechanic friend of mine calls them, "dummy lights." Recently the emblem on my dashboard lit up denoting that one of my tires had low air pressure. I didn't want to ignore the warning too long, lest I place not only myself, but also my entire family in jeopardy.

God has also placed a signal indicator light within each of his children, namely, the Holy Spirit. Spiritually speaking, it can be perilous to disregard your "Holy Spirit Admonition Indicator." Pay attention to your internal indicators (i.e., those subtle nudges of your conscience that tell you something is starting to go wrong). Get regular spiritual tune-ups.

Let's see what God's master mechanic Paul had to say about this:

> And do not grieve the Holy Spirit of God, by whom you were sealed for the day of redemption. Let all bitterness, wrath, anger, clamor, and evil speaking be put away from you, with all malice. And be kind to one another, tenderhearted, forgiving one another, just as God in Christ also forgave you.
>
> EPHESIANS 4:30–32, NKJV

> And do not grieve the Holy Spirit of God, with whom you were sealed for the day of redemption. Get rid of all bitterness, rage and anger, brawling and slander, along with every form of malice. Be

kind and compassionate to one another, forgiving each other, just as in Christ God forgave you.

EPHESIANS 4:30–32, NIV

WHEN THE SPIRIT SAYS, "OUCH"—F

- What does the word "grieve" mean (v. 30)?
- Is the Holy Spirit an impersonal force or a person (v. 30)?
- When is the actual "day of redemption" as referred to in verse 30?
- What's the difference between "wrath" and "anger" (v. 31)?
- What does the word "clamor" mean (v. 31)?
- Why is "evil speaking" coupled with "malice" (v. 31)?
- How vital is "forgiving one another" to our Christian walk (v. 32)?

WHEN THE SPIRIT SAYS, "OUCH"—I

The conjunction "and" appears at the beginning of our paragraph connecting the "put off" and "put on" admonitions of Ephesians 4:22–29 with the ministry of the Holy Spirit in Ephesians 4:30–32. Now that you see how this passage fuses with the previous one, mull over Paul's command in verse 30: "And do not grieve the Holy Spirit of God." To "grieve" means *to make sorrowful or sad*, ultimately *causing grief*. We "grieve the Holy Spirit of God" when we surrender to our old nature and practice "bitterness, wrath, anger, clamor, and evil speaking" (verse 31).

Observe specifically who is being grieved by these actions, "the Spirit, the Holy One of God" (the literal Greek translation). The original Greek emphasis lies upon the word "Holy," showing that the third member of the Trinity is absolutely pure and separated from sin. The Holy Spirit isn't an impersonal force, but a person. Notice the words "by whom"; this is not some detached spirit or thing (not "by which").

Paul then added, "You were sealed for the day of redemption." God "sealed" us with the Holy Spirit when we placed our faith in Jesus Christ.

As we learned from Ephesians 1:13–14, He will continue to dwell in us until Jesus returns on the day of redemption.

Since God's Spirit lives within us, Paul instructs, "Let all bitterness, wrath, anger, clamor, and evil speaking be put away from you, with all malice" (Eph. 4:31). "Bitterness" ranks number one on the things-that-must-go list. Aristotle defined bitterness as a resentful spirit that refuses reconciliation. The root idea of the word communicates *to cut* or *prick*.

Next Paul addresses "wrath and anger." "Wrath" refers to *an outburst from inward indignation* while "clamor" is translated as "brawling" in the NIV and speaks of the *yelling of an excited person*. "Evil speaking" can be translated as *blasphemy*. We could say that "clamor" describes verbal fist fighting, and "evil speaking" relates to an assault with words. When "with all malice" is appended to "clamor and evil speaking," the wickedness is intensified.

I'm sure you recall the importance of putting off your old nature and putting on the new. This is the same principle (vv. 31–32). In place of those sinful habits of verse 31, we are to "be kind to one another, tenderhearted, forgiving one another, just as God in Christ also forgave you" (v. 32). We are kind and tenderhearted when we provide for someone's needs compassiontely. "Forgiving one another" denotes *gracing* or *favoring* other people, graciously canceling out someone's sin against us.

WHEN THE SPIRIT SAYS, "OUCH"—R

Over decades of ministry a pastor does a lot of counseling. What sin do you think that I have had to deal with most often in a counseling session? It's bitterness. I am not surprised that Paul listed this life-wrecking sin as number one here. Countless times, I have counseled people whose lives have been altered by an inexcusable act, and while it is true that the perpetrators of harmful deeds will not escape their future accountability before the sovereign Lord, those who have been deeply wounded by a verbal or physical abuser can find healing by applying God's Word as a healing balm.

I'm not sure who originally said that bitterness is like drinking poison and waiting for the other person to die, but the statement rings true. How does bitterness set up shop in the heart of a child of God? It begins by not accepting the grace that our heavenly Father makes available to us every moment. Whenever a believer is attacked, either verbally or physically, God's grace and favor are accessible immediately. Look at how the early disciple Stephen (Acts 7) chose to welcome the supernatural ability of God (i.e. grace) even in the midst of being falsely accused and stoned to death. His parting words demonstrated the acceptance of God's grace when he needed it the most, "Lord, do not charge them with this sin" (Acts 7:60).

Hebrew 12:14–15 advises, "Pursue peace with all people, and holiness, without which no one will see the Lord: looking carefully lest anyone fall short of the grace of God; lest any root of bitterness springing up cause trouble, and by this many become defiled." Bitterness stems from not appropriating the grace of God. Once it sets in, it has a detrimental effect on everything.

Jesus taught his disciples to pray a prayer that we often call the Lord's Prayer. Matthew records this line: "And forgive us our debts, as we forgive our debtors" (Matt. 6:12). In the parallel passage in Luke's gospel, Luke replaced "debts" with "sins" (See Luke 11:4.) Perhaps the combined idea refers to forgiving "moral debts" or those who have hurt us morally. Not forgiving has very serious consequences. Here is how Jesus ended this important matter: "For if you forgive men their trespasses, your heavenly Father will also forgive you. But if you do not forgive men their trespasses, neither will your Father forgive your trespasses" (Matt. 6:14–15).

Friends, let's not focus upon the one who violated our life, but rather upon the One who granted us a full pardon for our sins. Which is the greater forgiveness, yours for the person who deeply wounded you, or Jesus' forgiveness of all your past, present, and future sin?

Another key passage on this vitally important topic is found a little further on in the Gospel of Matthew. Peter asked Jesus, "Lord, how often shall my brother sin against me, and I forgive him? Up to seven times?" (Matt. 18:21). Rabbis in Jesus' day taught that you should forgive the person who sinned against you three times. Peter felt that seven was an unimpeachably pious number.

Our Lord then rocked Peter's world with his response: "I do not say to you, up to seven times, but up to seventy times seven (Matt. 18:22), and then proceeded to tell a story to make the point that forgiveness should always be granted because we've been forgiven so much (Matt. 18:21–34). "So My heavenly Father also will do to you [punish you severely] if each of you, from his heart, does not forgive his brother his trespasses" (Matt. 18:35).

As we come back to Ephesians 4:32, let me ask you, are you harboring bitterness in your heart? If so, the only pathway to victory is to forgive the person who sinned against you, remembering how very much God has forgiven you. Consider again, "And be kind to one another, tenderhearted, forgiving one another, just as God in Christ also forgave you."

WHEN THE SPIRIT SAYS, "OUCH"—E

There exists no neutral territory for the child of God. Where the Holy Spirit is concerned, you are either grieving (paining) Him, or not. Our first employment point comes from Ephesians 4:30: *pain not God's Holy Spirit.* We follow through with this injunction when we refrain from sin, or repent of any of the sins mentioned in the following verse (or elsewhere).

The Holy Spirit resides within every child of God, and our ongoing personal relationship with Him depends upon holy living. "For God did not call us to uncleanness, but in holiness" wrote Paul in 1 Thessalonians 4:7, adding in verse 8: "Therefore he who rejects this does not reject man, but God, who has also given us His Holy Spirit."

Only a holy person can intimately know a holy God through His Spirit. That is why Jesus said, "Blessed are the pure in heart, for they shall see God" (Matt. 5:8). The writer of Hebrews concurs with, "Pursue peace with all men, and holiness, without which no one will see the Lord" (Heb. 12:14). The word "pursue" is translated elsewhere as *persecute.* In the same way that Saul, later known as Paul, persecuted Christians with the utmost of urgency, you should go after peace with all people and holiness with God. Again, the objective: *pain not God's Holy Spirit.*

Moving to the next verse (v. 31), our second application point is: *Put away bitterness and its allies.* This takes a deliberate initiative of the will. The way to avoid bringing sorrow and pain to the Holy Spirit is to set aside your bitterness once and for all. The third employment point rounds it out: *Put on kindness and imitate God's forgiveness* (Eph. 4:32).

Too often, I've witnessed how bitterness can take hold of a spouse's life when adultery by the other partner occurs. There was a married man who came to me and asked for an appointment to talk. We got together and this Christian man confessed that he'd been unfaithful to his wife. He had confessed his sin to God and pleaded for his wife's pardon. My heart ached for this precious couple who wanted so much to get past this ugly incident.

The overwhelmed woman desperately desired to have her marriage healed, but sadly she had allowed bitterness to fester. With both husband and wife in my study, I began to give them the biblical prescription for restoration, allowing the betrayed spouse to spend whatever time it would take to digest the relevant passages. Our first stop was Hebrews 12:14–16, to help the couple understand how grace not received results in bitterness. Our second station was the Lord's Prayer as given in Matthew 6:9–13, where we paid particular attention to, "For if you forgive men their trespasses, your heavenly Father will also forgive you. But if you do not forgive men their trespasses, neither will your Father forgive your trespasses" (vv. 14–15). Then, I quoted Ephesians 4:30–32, explaining that the way over this seemingly impossible hurdle comes from focusing, not upon the one who hurt you, but instead upon Jesus who pardoned you from all your sin. I pointed out that inasmuch as Jesus has erased an unpayable debt, then surely he or she who has been forgiven so much can pardon someone who has sinned against him or her.

Finally, we went to Mattew 18:21–35, the potent story of the two debtors, in which the one who was forgiven the most should grant a pardon to the less-indebted individual. I askd the hurt wife to take all those verses to a quiet place and to ponder them at length. I told her that once the full impact of God's enormous forgiveness had saturated her violated soul, she should tell God that she forgave her husband who had hurt her so badly, and then forgive her husband directly.

A few days later my telephone rang, and the wife said, "Pastor, I'm free.

I realize how awesome God's forgiveness is to me, so I forgave my husband." Perhaps you yourself will want to walk through this process and allow God to mend your heart permanently. He's waiting and willing!

CHAPTER FIFTEEN

How Do You Mimic the Invisible God?

EPHESIANS 5:1–12

⟿⟿

One day in the hospital, two little boys were lying on stretchers next to each other outside of the operating room. The first boy leaned over and asked, "What are you in for?"

The second boy replied, "I'm here to get my tonsils out and I'm nervous."

The first kid said, "You've got nothing to worry about! I had that done when I was four. They put you to sleep and when you wake up they give you lots of ice cream and Jell-O. It's a breeze!"

"Well what are you here for?" the second kid asked.

The first kid replied woefully. "A circumcision."

The second kid said, "Wow! That's bad. I had that done when I was born and I couldn't walk for a year!"

Certain conditions can make walking a challenge, and that includes our Christian walk, which is supposed to look like Jesus' walk. Ephesians 5:1–12 shows how earthbound saints like you and me can walk like our invisible God:

Therefore be followers of God as dear children. And walk in love, as Christ also has loved us and given Himself for us, an offering and a sacrifice to God for a sweet–smelling aroma. But fornication and all uncleanness or covetousness, let it not even be named among you, as is fitting for saints; neither filthiness, nor foolish talking, nor coarse jesting, which are not fitting, but rather giving

133

of thanks. For this you know, that no fornicator, unclean person, nor covetous man, who is an idolater, has any inheritance in the kingdom of Christ and God. Let no one deceive you with empty words, for because of these things the wrath of God comes upon the sons of disobedience. Therefore do not be partakers with them. For you were once darkness, but now you are light in the Lord. Walk as children of light (for the fruit of the Spirit is in all goodness, righteousness, and truth), proving what is acceptable to the Lord. And have no fellowship with the unfruitful works of darkness, but rather expose them. For it is shameful even to speak of those things which are done by them in secret.

EPHESIANS 5:1–12, NKJV

Therefore be imitators of God, as beloved children; and walk in love, just as Christ also loved you and gave Himself up for us, an offering and a sacrifice to God as a fragrant aroma. But immorality or any impurity or greed must not even be named among you, as is proper among saints; and there must be no filthiness and silly talk, or coarse jesting, which are not fitting, but rather giving of thanks. For this you know with certainty, that no immoral or impure person or covetous man, who is an idolater, has an inheritance in the kingdom of Christ and God. Let no one deceive you with empty words, for because of these things the wrath of God comes upon the sons of disobedience. Therefore do not be partakers with them; for you were formerly darkness, but now you are Light in the Lord; walk as children of Light (for the fruit of the Light consists in all goodness and righteousness and truth), trying to learn what is pleasing to the Lord. Do not participate in the unfruitful deeds of darkness, but instead even expose them; for it is disgraceful even to speak of the things which are done by them in darkness.

EPHESIANS 5:1–12, NASB

• What is the "therefore" there for (v. 1)?

WALK IN LOVE AND LIGHT—F

- What does the expression "followers of God" mean (v. 1)?
- What does "coarse jesting" mean (v. 4)?
- Why does verse 8 read, "you were once darkness," and not, "you were once *in the* darkness?"
- How does "proving what is acceptable to the Lord" differ from the traditional question often asked by young adults, "Why is this wrong" (v. 10)?
- How does Ephesians 5:11–12 relate to the background of the citizens of Ephesus?

WALK IN LOVE AND LIGHT—I

The "therefore" in verse 1 links Paul's theme of not grieving the Holy Spirit by putting off the old, and putting on the new (Eph. 4:30–32) with, "Be followers of God as dear children" (5:1), which lays the groundwork for the next few verses. "Be followers" is a command, and the word "followers" derives from the Greek word meaning *to mimic*. Paul is telling the Ephesians that they must *imitate* God as beloved sons and daughters.

A second imperative occurs in verse 2, "And walk in love." Who becomes the supreme model worthy of such imitation? Jesus Christ himself, of course: "…as Christ also has loved us and given Himself for us, an offering and a sacrifice to God for a sweet-smelling aroma (v. 2). Jesus' substitutionary atonement produced a beautiful fragrance before his Father's throne and it demonstrated how we should place others ahead of ourselves.

In order not to sully that perfect act of love, we need to avoid ungodliness on every level. Paul declared: "But fornication and all uncleanness or covetousness, let it not even be named among you, as is fitting for saints; neither filthiness, nor foolish talking, nor coarse jesting, which are not fitting" (vv. 3–4). These sins are the opposite of a sweet-smelling aroma. In fact, they repulse God. "Fornication" refers to both pre- and post-marital sex outside of wedlock, and it includes incest. The words "all uncleanness" point to any kind of ungodliness. "Covetousness" means a strong desire for the possessions of another, and this includes the unsanctioned partner desired by a fornicator or adulterer.

"Filthiness" includes base and foul language, and "foolish talking" literally translates as *moronic speech*. The English words "coarse jesting" derive from one Greek word used only once in the New Testament, a word which means *perverting one's speech to solicit laughter*. Filthiness, foolish talk, and coarse jesting should be replaced with the "giving of thanks," which expresses the right use of the tongue.

The apostle reminds the Ephesians that people who consistently practice these vices demonstrate an unregenerate nature (Eph. 5:5–6): "For this you know, that no fornicator, unclean person, nor covetous man, who is an idolater, has any inheritance in the kingdom of Christ and God. Let no one deceive you with empty words, for because of these things the wrath of God comes upon the sons of disobedience." The pronouncement, "sons of disobedience" is a Hebraism (an expression borrowed from the Hebrew language) that compares individuals who habitually exhibit these sins to the progeny of rebelliousness; in other words they are unsaved. Children of God shouldn't go back to their previous ways that included vile activities never sanctioned by God (v. 7).

Paul reminds the Ephesians of their former ways, "For you were once darkness, but now you are light in the Lord. Walk as children of light" (Eph. 5:8). Prior to believing in Jesus, the Ephesians used to not only live in darkness, blind to the truth, but they themselves *were* darkness.

Conversely, "But now you are light in the Lord" (Eph. 5:8b). In the same way, as children of God the believers are not only walking in the full daylight of the good news, they themselves *are* light. Therefore, Paul commands: "Walk as children of light."

The NKJV differs from the NASB in verse 9, where it uses the word "Spirit," derived from a majority of Greek manuscripts. The NASB uses "light," which arises from fewer, but older, Greek manuscripts. Either way, both "the Spirit" or "the light" come from God. (My personal belief is that "the Spirit" was what Paul originally wrote.)

By his very nature, God's Spirit will bring about "goodness, righteousness, and truth" (v. 9) in a believer. These three words denote active generosity, justice, doing what is right, and conducting one's life without deception.

Those who walk in God's light want to please God: "...proving what is acceptable to the Lord" (Eph. 5:10). The Greek verb for "proving" carries the idea of *testing for approval*. When I taught courses at a local Bible college, my goal for all the students was for them to pass the exam that I administered. They demonstrated their mastery of the material I had presented by doing well on the examination. As their teacher, I sincerely wanted them to pass the test.

What is acceptable to the Lord? (Eph. 5:10). The right question to ask about dubious activities should not be, "Why is this wrong?" but rather "Why is this right?" Consider Paul to have come from Missouri—the "Show Me State"—and telling the children of God, "Show me why this activity would please our heavenly Father."

The Lord had used Paul to reach these saints who had previously delved into satanic practices. On account of this he wrote, "And have no fellowship with the unfruitful works of darkness, but rather expose them. For it is shameful even to speak of those things which are done by them in secret" (Eph. 5:11–12). Now that they had been rescued from the Devil's grasp, they must not return to those dark pursuits. Their new light-filled mission gave them new marching orders: "Expose them." Now they were supposed to point their fingers at these godless undertakings to show that they were inherently wrong.

At the same time, obeying Paul's command to expose works of darkness was not supposed to include graphic descriptions of these despicable acts: "For it is shameful even to speak of those things which are done by them in secret" (Eph. 5:12). Nobody needs to have those images dancing around in his or her head.

WALK IN LOVE AND LIGHT—R

The first command, "Be followers" governs the rest of the passage. Paul practiced what he preached. In 1 Corinthians 4:16, he stated, "Therefore I urge you, imitate me." Later in the same book he reiterated, "Imitate me, just as I also imitate Christ" (1 Cor. 11:1). Is your life worthy of imitation? After all, people see you before they see Jesus. (Observe how Paul placed "us" before "the Lord" in 1 Thessalonians 1:6, "And you became followers of us and of the Lord...")

The command to "walk in love" (v. 2) is in the present tense and shows continual action. Jesus expects all believers to walk in love. When he evaluated the seven churches in Revelation 2–3, perhaps thirty years after Paul wrote the Epistle to the Ephesians, one of the seven churches was the church at Ephesus.

Jesus made one particular statement to each church: "I know your works." After these four piercing words are spoken in Revelation 2:2–3 to the church of Ephesus, he then gave a positive appraisal of their diligent labor, hatred of false doctrine, and patient perseverance in their labor for his name's sake. Then he pulls the rug out from under them: "Nevertheless I have this against you, that you have left your first love" (Rev. 2:4). Notice that Jesus didn't say, "you have *lost* your first love," but rather, "You have *left* your first love." The Ephesians had not misplaced their love for Jesus, but there had been a point of departure from him.

The Judge rendered his verdict on what had appeared, up to that point to have been a flawless church: "Remember therefore from where you have fallen; repent and do the first works, or else I will come to you quickly and remove your lampstand [their church] from its place—unless you repent" (Rev. 2:5). This abandonment of love had occurred even though Paul had given the earlier command to "walk in love" (Eph. 5:2.) Somewhere along the way it got ignored.

Sometimes I wonder how Jesus would judge the television and movie viewing habits of many Christians in our generation, considering how he condemned illicit thoughts along with the acts of fornication and adultery in Matthew 5:28. Consider your own viewing choices in light of Ephesians 5:3–4, "But fornication and all uncleanness or covetousness, let it not even be named among you, as is fitting for saints; neither filthiness, nor foolish talking, nor coarse jesting, which are not fitting."

Many years ago I attended a Bible conference with my family in Chicago. Once the convention ended, we stayed on at the hotel that had hosted our meetings. (Thankfully they extended the discounted convention rates to us!) One afternoon, I took my three sons Joshua, Daniel, and Kenny to the sunny, glass-enclosed, indoor swimming pool. I always enjoyed these special times with my boys, but it also gave my wife some much-needed quiet time.

We had been enjoying the swimming pool all to ourselves for a while when two middle-aged woman arrived. I can't fully explain it, but my Holy Spirit Admonition Indicator came on, and I knew that it was time to make a hasty exodus. Just as we exited, I could see that both women had planned on sunbathing—topless. I wonder how many children of God have ignored their Holy Spirit Admonition Indicator when it comes to television, movies, and DVDs?

Are we partakers of the very things we should be exposing as sin? To remain in the light we must "have no fellowship with the unfruitful works of darkness, but rather expose them. For it is shameful even to speak of those things which are done by them in secret" (Eph. 5:11–12).

WALK IN LOVE AND LIGHT—E

Remember the two hospitalized little boys at the start of this chapter who were awaiting their respective surgeries? The one lad was about to have a procedure that would inhibit his walking ability for a while. The following first employment point guides us in how to immediately and habitually walk with God: *imitate God by living in his love* (vv. 1–7). This combines the two commands given in Ephesians 5:1–2 ("be followers" and "walk in love").

Positively stated, to walk in God's love means to mimic Jesus, who pleased God by sacrificing his life for us; we must lay down our lives for our brothers and sisters in Christ. The vast majority of us will never have to die physically for someone else, but we can follow 1 John 3:16–17, which describes how we must yield our material possessions—they make up the substance of our physical existence—to meet the needs of our brethren: "By this we know love, because He laid down His life for us. And we also ought to lay down our lives for the brethren. But whoever has this world's goods, and sees his brother in need, and shuts up his heart from him, how does the love of God abide in him?"

This employment point should put you on the lookout to meet the needs of your family members in Christ. When God gives you that privilege, go for it. "Therefore, as we have opportunity," wrote Paul in Galatians 6:10, "let us do good to all, especially to those who are of the household of faith." *Imitate God by living in his love* by joyfully dispensing your money to provide for those who lack basic provisions.

To *imitate God by living in his love* is only possible if you tenaciously guard what goes into your mind that would provoke unclean living and speech (vv. 3–4). As Paul declared, "don't be partakers with them" (Eph. 5:7).

Specifically, I want you to write or print out Psalm 101:3 and place it above every television and computer screen that you own: "I will set nothing wicked [literally, "worthless"] before my eyes; I hate the work of *those* who fall away; it shall not cling to me." Interestingly, David concluded v. 4 with, "I will not know wickedness." The word "know" speaks of *intimate knowledge*. My beloved friends, God never created us to experience evil personally or through the eye gate into the mind. Apply these biblical truths consistently and you will *imitate God by living in His love.*

The second application point requires a similar amount of passion to please God: *Imitate God by living in his light* (vv. 8–12). God has graciously taken us from the grip of Satan and brought us into his spotless presence. Never forget, "For you were once darkness, but now you are light in the Lord, walk as children of light" (v. 8). We live in his light by allowing God's Spirit to produce "goodness, righteousness, and truth" (v. 9), while we prove what is acceptable to the Lord" (v. 10), and shun every dark path (vv. 11–12).

CHAPTER SIXTEEN

HEARING GOD'S ALARM CLOCK

EPHESIANS 5:13–17

—~∧∧∿~—

A woman walked up to a little old man rocking in a chair on his porch. "I couldn't help noticing how happy you look," she said. "What's your secret for a long happy life?"

"I smoke three packs of cigarettes a day," he said. "I also drink a case of whiskey a week, eat fatty foods, and never exercise."

"That's amazing," the woman said. "How old are you?"

"Twenty six," he said.

Christians should be skilled in "redeeming the time," walking day by day in the light of Christ. This is the message of our text for this chapter:

> But all things that are exposed are made manifest by the light, for whatever makes manifest is light. Therefore He says: "Awake, you who sleep, Arise from the dead, And Christ will give you light." See then that you walk circumspectly, not as fools but as wise, redeeming the time, because the days are evil. Therefore do not be unwise, but understand what the will of the Lord is.
>
> EPHESIANS 5:13–17, NKJV

> But all things being exposed by the light are made evident. For everything made evident is light, and for this reason it says: Awake, O sleeper! Rise from the dead, and Christ will shine on you! Therefore be very careful how you live—not as unwise but as wise, taking advantage of every opportunity, because the days are evil. For this reason do not be foolish, but be wise by understanding what the Lord's will is.
>
> EPHESIANS 5:13–17, NET

WAKE UP AND WALK WISELY—F

- What do the words "all things" point to (v. 13)?
- Why would Christians be told, "Arise from the dead" (v. 14) since they are already positionally raised with Jesus to the heavenly realms?
- What does it mean to "walk circumspectly" (v. 15)?
- How do you "redeem the time" as mentioned in verse 16?
- What did Paul mean when he wrote, "But understand what the will of the Lord is" (v. 17)?

WAKE UP AND WALK WISELY—I

The "all things" in Ephesians 5:13 refers to the secret sins of the unrighteous in the previous verse. Those darkened deeds (in which the Ephesians also participated before their salvation) were to be shunned, and not even described or discussed. Paul then went on to write, "All things [the secret sins] that are exposed are made manifest by the light." "Exposed" (also used back in verse 11) means *to convict, and prove that an individual is guilty of the accusation, and should be shamed.* Light reveals the heinous nature of these activities, "for whatever makes manifest is light."

Next Paul apparently took two Old Testament verses, Isaiah 26:19 and 60:1, and combined them into Ephesians 5:14; some people believe this is a verse from an ancient Christian hymn. The command, "Awake, you who sleep" urges people to arise from their sluggishness. ("Sleep" in this context does not mean napping, but rather yielding to sloth or indifference.) Paul added, "Arise from the dead," because it was important not to revert (as some apparently did) to their previous spiritual dead behavior if they were to receive the light of Christ. The future tense verb "will give" speaks of Jesus illuminating the believer's path once he or she chooses to leave the life of Christian complacency for one of active obedience.

Another command appears in verse 15: "See then that you walk circumspectly, not as fools but as wise." To walk "circumspectly," one undertakes the Christian journey *carefully, accurately,* and *diligently.* Indeed, the saints must comport themselves "not as fools [unwise people] but as wise."

What does it mean to live wisely? Verse 16 explains: "...[by] redeeming the time, because the days are evil." "Redeeming" conveys the idea of *buying up*, and the thing to purchase, according to Paul, is "the time," which could be translated "the season," referring to *a fixed or definite period*. We need to make the most of every hour of every day, living in obedience to God's commands.

Paul concluded this section with, "Therefore do not be unwise, but understand what the will of the Lord *is*" (Eph. 5:17). The word "unwise" here is a different Greek word than was translated by "fools" in verse 15; here the expression means *without the mind*. We could use the modern expression "a no brainer."

Finally, Paul exhorted the Ephesians: ". . . but understand what the will of the Lord is." In this context, what is God's will? It consists of awakening from spiritual laziness, and living wisely by using every opportunity (time or occasion) that God provides for you.

WAKE UP AND WALK WISELY—R

God's light powerfully exposes the filth of sin. Paul, who had personally experienced the piercing rays of God's light at his conversion (Acts 9), testified here to its strength. He wrote, "But all things that are exposed are made manifest by the light, for whatever makes manifest is light" (Eph. 5:13). We will allow the story of the woman taken in adultery (John 8:1–12) to further illuminate this verse.

Jesus went to the temple very early one morning (possibly before dawn) to teach the Word of God (John 8:2). "Then the scribes and Pharisees brought to Him a woman caught in adultery. And when they had set her in the midst, they said to Him, 'Teacher, this woman was caught in adultery, in the very act'" (John 8:3–4). They were trying to justify punishing her by stoning (Deut. 22:22–24) and they were hoping to catch Jesus between the regulations of Moses and the secular government of Rome.

Our Lord then did something that seemed irrational. "Jesus stooped down and wrote on the ground with His finger, as though He did not hear"

(John 8:6b). The self-righteous religious leaders persisted in their quest to entrap Jesus. "So when they continued asking Him, He raised Himself up and said to them, 'He who is without sin among you, let him throw a stone at her first?'" (John 8:7).

Jesus, the giver of the Law, allowed its reproving power to work. John 8:9 continues, "Then those who heard it, being convicted by their conscience, went out one by one, beginning with the oldest even to the last." Why did the oldest leave first? They had accumulated more sin over their long lives and therefore experienced greater guilt.

After everyone had filed out, Jesus remained alone with the woman. He then asked two penetrating questions: "'Woman, where are those accusers of yours? Has no one condemned you?'" (John 8:10). She responded, "'No one, Lord.' And Jesus said to her, 'Neither do I condemn you; go and sin no more'" (John 8:11).

God's Holy Word reveals sin. This story began before the sun arose, but having been ushered into the very presence of the light of life, the woman left in the brightness of a new day. "Then Jesus spoke to them again, saying, 'I am the light of the world. He who follows Me shall not walk in darkness, but have the light of life'" (John 8:12).

In the same way, Paul advised the Ephesians to "walk circumspectly, not as fools, but as wise" (Eph. 5:15). The word "circumspectly" occurs also in Matthew 2:8, where it has been translated as "diligently." (This is the narrative about Herod pretending to the Magi that he had a sincere interest in finding the Messiah. "And he [Herod] sent them [the wise men or magi] to Bethlehem and said, 'go and search diligently for the young child.'")

Paul further augmented his case for wise living with the exhortation, "redeeming the time, because the days are evil" (Eph. 5:16). There are two basic words for "time" in the Greek New Testament. One deals with the succession of minutes, which gives us the English word "chronology." The other Greek term, used here, can be translated as "season," and it refers to a period of opportunity. Consider how it occurs in Galatians 6:10: "Therefore, as we have opportunity, let us do good to all, especially to those who are of the household of faith." In essence, Paul was telling the Ephesians to take advantage of all opportunities to serve God because a wicked world might rob them of future occasions to serve the Lord. "Therefore," he tells them, "do not be unwise, but understand what the will of the Lord is" (v. 17). The saints should "wake up" and avail themselves of every chance to serve the Lord because who knows how long that window of opportunity might last.

WAKE UP AND WALK WISELY—E

It's time to apply what we have learned in these verses. Our first employment point from Ephesians 5:13–14 is this: *Wake up spiritually to receive light.* God doesn't want Christians sleeping on the job, because it keeps them in the dark.

Christians have the biblical obligation to avoid and expose works of darkness. We can't do that if we're asleep spiritually. This explains why Paul commanded the Ephesians, "Awake, you who sleep" (Eph. 5:14). As we learned earlier, the word "sleep" refers to *spiritual indifference or lethargy.* That same Greek term occurs three times in 1 Thessalonians 5:5–10. Are you awake, or asleep? Is God's alarm clock going off in your life?

Our second application point flows logically from the first one: *Walk wisely to comprehend God's will* (from Eph. 5:15–17). To bolster this truth read Jesus' words: "He who follows Me shall not walk in darkness, but have the light of life" (John 8:12). Individuals who "walk circumspectly, not as fools but as wise, redeeming the time, because the days are evil" will "understand what the will of the Lord is" (Eph. 5:15–17). When you walk with Jesus, you cannot remain in the darkness.

Discovering the will of God for your life is simpler than you might imagine. Where should you go to school? What vocation should you pursue? Whom should you marry? Practice the known will of God as revealed in the Bible (in Eph. 5:13–17, for example), and the sovereign Lord of the universe, in His good time, will lead you according to his will. God delights to guide his children.

CHAPTER SEVENTEEN

THE BENEFITS OF THE SPIRIT-FILLED LIFE

EPHESIANS 5:18–21

⸺∿⌁⸺

At a New Year's party at the end of 1906, Mark Twain play-acted getting drunk as he delivered a fake lecture on temperance. Apparently he was quite convincing in both roles.

Paul did not have to play-act in order to get his point across in Ephesians 5:18–21, and his words were even more convincing—and convicting—than Twain's:

> And do not be drunk with wine, in which is dissipation, but be filled with the Spirit, speaking to one another in psalms and hymns and spiritual songs, singing and making melody in your heart to the Lord, giving thanks always for all things to God the Father in the name of our Lord Jesus Christ, submitting to one another in the fear of God.
>
> EPHESIANS 5:18–21, NKJV

> Don't destroy yourself by getting drunk, but let the Spirit fill your life. When you meet together, sing psalms, hymns, and spiritual songs, as you praise the Lord with all your heart. Always use the name of our Lord Jesus Christ to thank God the Father for everything. Honor Christ and put others first.
>
> EPHESIANS 5:18–21, CEV

SPIRIT-FILLED LIVING—F

- Why is Spirit-filled living mentioned with the negative example of drunkenness (v. 18)?
- How does one become filled with God"s Holy Spirit (v. 18)?
- What are the three evidences of being filled with the Holy Spirit (vv. 19–21)?

SPIRIT-FILLED LIVING—I

Why introduce Spirit-filled living with the negative example of drunkenness (v. 18)? Let me offer two possibilities. The pre-Christian lives of some of the Ephesians had been characterized by drunkenness. Even those who did not have that problem could easily understand the contrast between being controlled by alcohol and being filled with the Spirit.

From Genesis to Revelation, the Bible does not condemn drinking, but rather drunkenness. (Even when the Bible forbids strong drink, such as was the case for the Nazirites in Numbers 6, this is the exception and not the rule.) Accordingly, Paul commands believers, "Do not be drunk with wine," adding, "in which is dissipation." The original Greek word translated "dissipation" suggests *no hope of safety*. In other words, no security comes by submitting to the destabilizing influence of wine.

Then Paul offered the believers' alternative: "but be filled with the Spirit." The word "filled" conveys volumes about our walk with God. To begin with, the verb "filled" implies *to be controlled*. Second, the verb as an imperative tells the believers what they must do. As alcohol controls the inebriated person, so now let the Spirit govern you. Third, "filled" is a present tense verb, which shows that the believer should be under the Spirit's control continuously. Fourth, the passive voice (which indicates that some outside agent acts upon the verb) testifies that believers are to allow or submit to this continual filling.

Three results come from the Spirit's filling—joy, thankfulness, and submissiveness (vv. 19–21). Spirit-filled saints overflow with the joy of the Lord (see v. 19). In their singing and making melody in psalms and hymns and spiritual songs, the Spirit-filled Ephesians would have used everything from the Book of Psalms, Israel's songbook, to spontaneous songs of worship. With grateful hearts, they trusted completely in the One who governs the universe, and they could praise God through any circumstance, "giving thanks always for all things" (v. 20).

Submissiveness was the natural result, and the Spirit-filled Ephesian believers were freely "submitting to one another in the fear of God" (v. 21). The Greek word for "submit" means *to arrange under,* and it occurs forty times in the Greek New Testament. When we submit to our fellow Christians or submit to any member of the Trinity (even as the members of the Godhead submit to each other), we please the Father; in essence, we have "arranged" ourselves under Him.

SPIRIT-FILLED LIVING—R

Jesus' first miracle as recorded in John 2 consisted of turning water into wine for a wedding celebration, which indicates an endorsement for fermented beverages. But just because Christians have the liberty to drink, should they? The Bible offers sage advice about this question.

Noah brought shame to himself and his family because of his lack of discretion. In the first reference to wine in the Bible, Genesis 9:20–21 reports, "And Noah began to be a farmer, and he planted a vineyard. Then he drank and was drunk, and became uncovered in his tent." God has high standards when it comes to his dedicated servants. As we saw earlier (Num. 6), Nazirites were forbidden to drink wine. In the New Testament, elders and deacons were expected to maintain sobriety. Paul, writing to Timothy, who pastored in Ephesus, advised that deacons should be "not given to much wine" (1 Tim. 3:8).

One of the reasons I've personally chosen not to drink any alcohol is to keep others from being tripped up by my example: "It is good neither to eat meat nor drink wine, nor do anything by which your brother stumbles or is offended or is made weak" (Rom. 14:21). I've joked with my congregation that I haven't caused a car accident since I've had my license, or done any drinking since I reached the legal age. However, since I didn't become a Christian until age sixteen, I've had some experiences that have enabled me to personally experience the negative effects of alcohol. For this reason, along with my desire to be a good witness, my wife and I have raised our three sons in an alcohol-free home.

It should be observed that to be filled with the Spirit means to be controlled by the Spirit. I like to compare the Spirit's filling to fans watching a baseball game. When my three adult sons were younger, they loved baseball. Kim and I loved taking them to a major league game each season. At each game an essential purchase was made—each of the three boys would be given the official program with scorecard. By the ripe old age of seven, these youngsters were keeping the stats verbatim; they didn't miss recording one single pitch.

Imagine our conservative family being surrounded by other fans from the outset of the game—watching them transform from tranquil fans into boisterous (drunk) ones. They would start by flagging the beer man for "refreshment." Eventually, during the seventh inning stretch, when a song would be played over the loudspeakers as the fans stood, inevitably the ones who had been drinking would be swinging and swaying to the rhythm of the song. They were now controlled by the alcohol.

My friend, your joy shouldn't come from a bottle, but from the One who sent his Son to die for your sin. Our songs should arise from a joy-filled life because of the Spirit's presence. Strive to make Ephesians 5:18–19 a reality in your life: "And do not be drunk with wine, in which is dissipation; but be filled with the Spirit, speaking to one another in psalms and hymns and spiritual songs, singing and making melody in your heart to the Lord."

The heart of a Spirit-filled child of God overflows with thankfulness because he or she knows that God can be trusted always. Paul, who on more than one occasion spent time in dirty and dank prisons, nevertheless wrote, "Rejoice always, pray without ceasing, in everything give thanks; for this is the will of God in Christ Jesus for you" (1 Thess. 5:16–18).

Besides trusting God, a third result of being Spirit-filled is submitting to Him. Sadly, the word "submission" has fallen upon tough times. Yet, one notable by-product of the Spirit's filling consists of "submitting to one another in the fear of God" (v. 21). To whom should Spirit-filled believers humbly submit? For one, to parents. Jesus yielded himself to his parents (Luke 2:51–52). Imagine that, the omniscient Son of God put himself under the authority of his humble earthly parents.

Christians are subject to the laws of the land and should yield themselves to their respective governments. 1 Peter 2:13–14 states, "Therefore submit yourselves to every ordinance of man for the Lord's sake, whether to the king as supreme, or to governors, as to those who are sent by him for the punishment of evildoers and for the praise of those who do good."

Furthermore, younger people should submit to older ones, and church members should submit to their pastors: "Likewise you younger people, submit yourselves to your elders. Yes, all of you be submissive to one another, and be clothed with humility, for 'God resists the proud, But gives grace to the humble'" (1 Pet. 5:5).

The same verb for "submit" appears in James 4:7—"Therefore submit to God. Resist the devil and he will flee from you." When we align ourselves under God's authority structure, our submission deprives Satan of access to our lives.

SPIRIT-FILLED LIVING—E

The filling ministry of the Holy Spirit differs from the baptizing ministry of the Holy Spirit. The latter occurs once at salvation: "For by one Spirit we were all baptized into one body—whether Jews or Greeks, whether slaves or free—and have all been made to drink into one Spirit" (1 Cor. 12:13, see also Acts 2:4.). Unlike the one-time Spirit baptism of the believer at salvation, the filling work of the Spirit should be experienced regularly, and that is why Paul and others enjoin repeatedly, "be filled," and that's what happened post-Pentecost: "And when they had prayed, the place where they were assembled together was shaken; and they were all filled with the Holy Spirit, and they spoke the word of God with boldness" (Acts 4:31). This explains why Paul used the present-tense verb when he wrote in Ephesians 5:18, "Be filled with the Spirit."

That is our employment point: *Be filled with the Spirit.* Remember that "be filled" is something that happens to you because you permit him to control you. You cannot fill yourself with the Spirit. You must constantly and completely depend upon his leading, as Jesus did: "Then Jesus, being filled with the Holy Spirit, returned from the Jordan and was led by the Spirit into the wilderness" (Luke 4:1). Moreover, submit to the authority of God's Word: "Let the word of Christ dwell in you richly" (Col. 3:16). As tea becomes stronger when the tea bag steeps, so you must be saturated with the living Word in order to be filled.

CHAPTER EIGHTEEN

FOLLOW THE LEADER AND LOVE THE FOLLOWER

EPHESIANS 5:22–23

⌐∿∿⌐

Socrates the philosopher said: "By all means marry. If you get a good wife, you will become happy; if you get a bad one, you will become a philosopher—and that is also good." I'm not going to ask you if you are happily married or a philosopher! Paul's guidance for married couples didn't derive from mere observation, but from the revealed Word of God. Let's consider his prescription for a God-centered marriage that is based upon Spirit-filled living:

> Wives, submit to your own husbands, as to the Lord. For the husband is head of the wife, as also Christ is head of the church; and He is the Savior of the body. Therefore, just as the church is subject to Christ, so let the wives be to their own husbands in everything.
>
> Husbands, love your wives, just as Christ also loved the church and gave Himself for it, that He might sanctify and cleanse it with the washing of water by the word, that He might present it to Himself a glorious church, not having spot or winkle or any such thing, but that it should be holy and without blemish. So husbands ought to love their own wives as their own bodies; he who loves his wife loves himself. For no one ever hated his own flesh, but nourishes and cherishes it, just as the Lord does the church. For we are members of His body, of His flesh and of His bones. "For this reason a man shall leave his father and mother and be joined to his wife, and the two shall become one flesh." This is a great mystery, but I speak concerning Christ and the

church. Nevertheless let each one of you in particular so love his own wife as himself, and let the wife see that she respects her husband.

EPHESIANS 5:22–33, NKJV

Wives, submit to your husbands as to the Lord. For the husband is the head of the wife as Christ is the head of the church, his body, of which he is the Savior. Now as the church submits to Christ, so also wives should submit to their husbands in everything.

Husbands, love your wives, just as Christ loved the church and gave himself up for her to make her holy, cleansing her by the washing with water through the word. and to present her to himself as a radiant church, without stain or wrinkle or any other blemish, but holy and blameless. In this same way, husbands ought to love their wives as their own bodies. He who loves his wife loves himself. After all, no one ever hated his own body, but he feeds and cares for it, just as Christ does the church—for we are members of his body. "For this reason a man will leave his father and mother and be united to his wife, and the two will become one flesh." This is a profound mystery—but I am talking about Christ and the church. However, each one of you also must love his wife as he loves himself, and the wife must respect her husband.

EPHESIANS 5:25–33, NIV

SPIRIT-FILLED MARRIAGE—F

- Does the wife's submission to the husband (v. 22) show that she's inferior to him?
- What are the biblical reasons for wives submitting to their husbands?
- Are there any exceptions listed in verse 24 to wives submitting to their husbands?
- Why is Jesus and his sacrifice for the church the example that

husbands should apply when it comes to loving their wives (v. 25)?

- What picture are Christian husbands to portray to the world, according to Ephesians 5:26–29?
- What are Christian marriages to display to the world, according to Ephesians 5:30–33?

SPIRIT-FILLED MARRIAGE—I

Paul's first imperative in these verses, "Wives, submit to your own husbands, as to the Lord" (v. 22) follows on the heels of the third result of being Spirit-filled from the previous verse, "...submitting to one another in the fear of God" (v. 21). The same verb "submit" occurs in both verses, and it means *to arrange under.*

Why should the wife arrange herself under her husband's lead? "For the husband is head of the wife" (v. 22). And, Paul added, because "as also Christ is head of the church; and He is also Savior of the body" (v. 23). The wife should follow her husband's lead because of the Lordship of Christ.

Paul tied these concepts together in verse 24: "Therefore, just as the church is subject to Christ, so let the wives be to their own husbands in everything." Only by the Spirit's inner strengthening can a wife yield to her husband in every matter. The ideal biblical marriage consists of a wife who is governed by the Holy Spirit's equipping, and who has a husband similarly directed by his lead; when both are Spirit-filled, she can joyfully submit to his supervision. The perfect balance for marriage occurs when wives willingly follow their husbands, and when husbands lovingly lead their wives.

"Husbands, love your wives" (v. 25), writes Paul, using the familiar Greek word, *agape.* This verb appears 142 times in the New Testament and it indicates a kind of love that finds joy in serving another. Husbands are to love their wives "just as Christ also loved the church and gave Himself for it." Husbands must be willing to lay down their lives for their wives as Jesus sacrificially gave himself for us. A husband who carries this disposition will make it far easier for his wife to yield to his leadership.

Jesus laid down his life for the church, first, so that the church might be sanctified (*set apart*) as his special possession. Paul wrote, "...that He might sanctify and cleanse it with the washing of water by the word" (v. 26). To "cleanse it with the washing of water by the word" is a metaphor for the washing of regeneration.

Second, Jesus laid down his life for the church so "that He might present it to Himself a glorious church, not having spot or wrinkle or any such thing," and third, "that it should be holy and without blemish" (v. 27). Like a bride dressed in white (as a testimony to moral purity) on the wedding day, the church should mirror Christ in marriage.

Paul showed how husbands should imitate Jesus: "So husbands ought to love their own wives as their own bodies; he who loves his wife loves himself" (v. 28). Just as Jesus loves the church, which is his body, husbands must love their wives; the two are now one. Paul appealed to a self-evident truth, that men naturally care for themselves (v. 29): "For no one ever hated his own flesh, but nourishes and cherishes it, just as the Lord does the church." In the same way that husbands have regard for their bodies, Jesus looks after the church, which is his body.

The reason Christ holds the church in such high esteem becomes manifest, for we are living parts of his body. Paul quotes Adam (from Genesis 2:23) in the middle of verse 30: "For we are members of His body, of His flesh and of His bones." The church is Christ's own body; this is why he loves her so much. The first man, Adam, realized at Eve's creation that she was to become one with him. Paul now quotes in verse 31 a foundational passage for every marriage: "For this reason a man shall leave his father and mother and be joined to his wife, and the two shall become one flesh" (Gen. 2:24). It seems that this "one flesh" relationship is what Paul had in mind as he wrote this passage. The married couple should leave their parents and permanently cleave to one another, enjoying the highest form of intimacy.

God has granted Christian marriages the sacred privilege of displaying the magnificent portrait of Christ's love for the church. As Paul marveled at God's plan, he wrote, "This is a great mystery, but I speak concerning Christ and the church" (v. 33). Once hidden from previous generations, this profound picture of Christian husbands and wives, filled by God's Holy

Spirit and revealing Jesus' deep love for the church, makes visible the invisible love Jesus has for his body.

In conclusion, Paul wrote, "Nevertheless let each one of you in particular so love his own wife as himself, and let the wife see that she respects her husband" (v. 33). Once again, the perfect balance to marriage is given through two commands. The husband must have the highest form of love for his wife, and she must look up to him.

Clearly, Paul based much of what he wrote in Ephesians 5:22–33 from other Scriptures. Let's see how it all fits together.

SPIRIT-FILLED MARRIAGE—R

What is biblical submission? As we have seen, the word "submit" means *to arrange under.* In order for a person (wife or otherwise) to submit to another, he or she must first yield his or her will to God. With this humble presentation to God comes the filling of the Spirit and divine enablement.

The apostle James made a series of imperative statements to underline the importance of submission, beginning with: "Therefore submit to God" (James 4:7). The reason for the submission is stated in the previous verse: "God resists the proud, but gives grace to the humble."

Does submission imply inferiority? No! Jesus, in his youth, submitted to his parents. Luke 2:51 reports, "Then He went down with them and came to Nazareth, and was subject to them." The submission of the eternal Son of God to his earthly parents did not indicate his inferiority, but rather his willingness to submit to His heavenly Father, and his continued obedience to his will.

Carefully observe how 1 Corinthians 11:3 bears the truth not only that male headship comes from the priority of creation—Adam was created before Eve—but that submission doesn't imply a second-class status: "But I want you to know that the head of every man is Christ, the head of woman is man [the priority of creation], and the head of Christ is God." When the second member of the Godhead yielded himself to the Father, his humility didn't betray imperfection, but more precisely an understanding of God's divine order.

Must the wife yield to her husband in every situation that might arise? After all, didn't Paul write, "in everything" wives are to submit to their husbands (v. 24)? There exists an exception to the rule; it is when the husband desires his wife to follow his lead in a way that will cause her to violate God's Word. For instance, when government officials forbade the apostles to preach (Acts 5), which was a clear breach of Jesus' command for them to proclaim the gospel to every person (Mark 16:15), note that the leader of the apostles, Peter, stated, "We ought to obey God rather than men" (in Acts 5:29). Peter and the others would keep on preaching, because they had a higher obligation to God than to the government. Wives, as with anyone under authority, should not obey when their husbands tell them to disobey the clear teachings of God's Word.

The Christian husband, after all, has been commanded to love his wife "just as Christ also loved the church and gave Himself for it" (v. 25). What does this kind of love look like? Paul furnished us with that beautiful chapter on love in his letter to the Corinthian church. The husband's love for his wife can be found here, beginning with 1 Corinthians 13:4—"Love suffers long and is kind." Doesn't that beautifully recount how Jesus cared for his apostles? As they were debating who would be the greatest in the kingdom, Jesus suffered long with their self-centeredness, and then he washed their feet, demonstrating kindness to them. The apostle of love, John, elegantly captures Jesus' disposition toward his disciples: "Having loved His own who were in the world, He loved them to the end" (John 13:1). He loved them with all His holy being.

A husband who aspires to honor God's Word and "love his wife as Christ loved the church" will vigorously pursue practicing 1 Corinthians 13:4–8. He cannot lose if he does so, because "love never fails" (1 Cor. 13:8).

SPIRIT-FILLED MARRIAGE—E

I believe it is important to remind you that the application of this section of Scripture remains unattainable without your being Spirit-filled. Our first employment point would be impossible otherwise: *Wife, follow your husband.* I know that these words are easy to write, but difficult to practice because, in reality, all submission to authorities remains challenging because of our indwelling sin nature.

God had given Adam the privilege and awesome responsibility of leading his wife. Yet when the chips were down (or the fruit was pointed out), he followed his wife instead of God and sinned with his eyes wide open. When God intervened, he said to Eve: "Your desire shall be for your husband, and he shall rule over you" (Gen. 3:16). One of the consequences of the fall was that woman would desire to rule their husbands, which is contrary to the principles of God's creation.

On account of this inclination, the wife must humbly submit to Christ and yield to the leadership of her husband by the Spirit's power. Wives, memorize Ephesians 5:18–24 and ask the indwelling Holy Spirit to help you internalize that passage.

And then, as I turn to the husbands, you wives don't need to feel you need to sharpen your elbows in order to poke your husbands in the ribs; let me do the prodding for you! Employment point number two won't be a surprise to anybody: *Husbands, adore your wives.* I use the word "adore" because it means to love and respect someone deeply. Your mandate, no less challenging than the one given to wives, must also be carried out by means of the dual action of God's Word and his Spirit. As an important part of your employment, memorize and internalize 1 Corinthians 13:4–8a. And remember: "Love never fails."

Our third employment point should give both husbands and wives the incentive to follow through on their earlier assignments. Based upon Ephesians 5:30–33, *godly marriages reflect our oneness with Christ.* The earthy relationship of "one flesh" between Christian husband and wife becomes the channel whereby we reveal Christ in us to the world. God deserves all the glory we can offer him, and this becomes our sacred privilege to manifest Jesus through our godly marriages.

Ephesians 5:22–33 is both spiritually rich and extremely simple. When husbands love their wives as Jesus loved the church, and when wives follow their husbands' lead, then those godly marriages will reflect their oneness with Christ and God is glorified. Remember, it all begins with being Spirit-filled!

CHAPTER NINETEEN

ONLY THE GOOD DIE YOUNG?

EPHESIANS 6:1–4

~~∧∧~~

I grew up in the 1970s. A song that describes the moral decay of that era was written by Billy Joel and appeared in 1977. The title of the song was *Only the Good Die Young*.

Is that true? Do only the good die young? Paul, who wrote by the inspiration of the Holy Spirit, wouldn't agree. Here's how I know:

> Children, obey your parents in the Lord, for this is right. "Honor your father and mother," which is the first commandment with promise: "that it may be well with you and you may live long on the earth." And you, fathers, do not provoke your children to wrath, but bring them up in the training and admonition of the Lord.
>
> EPHESIANS 6:1–4, NKJV

> Children, obey your parents in the Lord, for this is right. "Honor your father and mother (which is the first commandment with a promise), so that it may be well with you, and that you may live long on the earth." Fathers, do not provoke your children to anger, but bring them up in the discipline and instruction of the Lord.
>
> EPHESIANS 6:1–4, NASB

SPIRIT-FILLED CHILDREN & FATHERS—F

- Is the Greek term for "obey" in Ephesians 6:1 the same word as the one translated as "submit" in Ephesians 5:22?
- What does the word "honor" mean (v. 2)?

- Ephesians 6:2 specifies that honoring your parents, which is the fifth of the ten commandments in Exodus 20, "is the first commandment with promise." Yet doesn't the second commandment about idolatry also have a promise? Does this show Paul's statement to be incorrect?
- How do fathers provoke their children to anger as stated in Ephesians 6:4?
- What do the words "training" and "admonition" mean in Ephesians 6:4?

SPIRIT-FILLED CHILDREN & FATHERS—I

Paul began this section by addressing the children directly. The fact that the apostle engaged them categorically implies that they were old enough to understand the instructions given. They, like the husbands and wives (their parents), also needed to humbly submit to the Lord so that the Spirit could work through them, producing obedience to God's Word.

Paul commanded them to "obey your parents in the Lord" (v. 1). The Greek word for "obey" differs from the verb "submit" studied in the previous section. This term, "obey," conveys the idea of *hearing under*. This is more than mere biological hearing, because it includes the idea of listening and heeding the parents' direction. For children to obey their parents is the same as submitting to the Lord since He put the child under the parents' authority. In Paul's time as well as in our own, so many youngsters are doing what is wrong. Paul gave a basic reason why children should yield to their parents' wishes; "for this is right."

Not only are children to obey their parents, they should also honor them. Ephesians 6:2–3 notes a particular blessing that comes to children who observe the Old Testament instruction to honor their parents: "'Honor your father and mother,' which is the first commandment with promise: 'that it may be well with you and you may live long on the earth.'" To "honor" means to *value, esteem,* or *cherish*. The children who value, esteem, and cherish their parents will be granted God's blessings ("it may be well with you") and promised a long life ("you may live long on the earth").

Next, Paul matter-of-factly confronts the fathers: "And you, fathers, do not provoke your children to wrath, but bring them up in the training and admonition of the Lord" (Eph. 6:4). Fathers are not to move their children to the point of anger by their autocratic, insensitive, or unjust requirements. Instead, they should "bring them up in the training and admonition of the Lord." They must nurture them carefully, instructing and disciplining them wisely, giving them verbal warnings as needed. Spirit-filled fathers should, in love, apply both the rod and wise reproof to their children.

Paul imparts profound biblical truths to both children and parents here, and much of what he shared came from the Old Testament.

SPIRIT-FILLED CHILDREN & FATHERS—R

As I mentioned above, "obey" means *to hear under*, which conveys the concept of complying with the wishes of another. To look at an incident that happened to Jesus and his disciples, even inanimate objects—or the weather—can obey a higher authority. The story is found in the eighth chapter of the Gospel of Matthew. Terrified when their boat was caught in a horrendous storm, Jesus' followers were awed when his spoken words immediately calmed the winds and the sea. They queried, "Who can this be, that even the winds and the sea obey Him?" (Matt. 8:27). The elements of nature fully submitted to his rebuke.

The children who value their parents and submit to their verbal commands are told about "the first commandment with promise: 'that it may be well with you and you may live long on the earth'" (Eph. 6:2–3). However, doesn't the earlier commandment number two also carry a promise, which would show Paul's statement to be inaccurate? In Exodus 20:4–6 those who create a carved image to worship are told, "For I, the Lord your God, am a jealous God, visiting the iniquity of the fathers on the children to the third and fourth generations of those who hate Me, but showing mercy to thousands, to those who love Me and keep My commandments." Shouldn't this be considered the first commandment with a promise?

True, this second of the ten commandments of Moses carries a general promise—namely that idolatry causes God to visit the iniquity of the fathers upon the children for three or four generations. But the difference between the second and the fifth commandment is that the fifth commandment's promise is specific to the child who honors his parents: "…that it may be well with you, and you may live long on the earth." Paul is calling the fifth commandment the first one with a well-defined promise.

Does this guarantee that every child who honors his parents will have a long life? Of course not. Many times, God will permit a child who yields to and honors his parents not to live to become a senior saint. Even our Lord Jesus would be an exception to the fifth commandment's promise if it were interpreted to guarantee long life! He clearly bowed to his parents' guidance (see Luke 2), and yet, according to the sovereignty of God, he died before the age of forty.

And yet God's Word gives other examples of those who did not honor their parents and they suffered the consequences, for example Nadab and Abihu (Lev. 10:1–9), the two older sons of Aaron, who perished for their disobedience to God and their blatant disrespect for Aaron, who was both their father and high priest. A similar example would be the priests Hophni and Phineas, the disobedient sons of Eli the high priest at Shiloh, who also died prematurely (see 1 Samuel 2–4).

"Fathers, do not provoke your children to wrath," wrote the apostle Paul in Ephesians 6:4. To "provoke to wrath" carries the idea of poking or prodding a child, leading to irritation. It is the opposite of encouragement. Paul addressed fathers directly also in Colossians 3:21, "Fathers, do not provoke your children, lest they become discouraged." As the head of the home, a father is supposed to build up his children spiritually, never to tear them down. Paul added in the same verse, "but bring them up in the training and admonition of the Lord." Biblical training of children requires a two-pronged approach, training and admonition.

You may recall that "training" originally meant instruction and came to include discipline. Appropriate training provides three benefits: love, legitimacy, and likeness.

The word "training" occurs six times in the Greek New Testament, four times within chapter 12 of the Book of Hebrews (vv. 5, 7, 8, 11.) In Heb. 12:5, the writer quotes from Proverbs 3:11–12, "My son, do not despise the chastening [training] of the Lord, nor be discouraged when you are rebuked by Him." Verse 6 goes on to say, "For whom the Lord loves He chastens, and scourges every son whom He receives." By this we see that training displays not only God's love for us, but also a father's love for his son or daughter.

Hebrews 12:7–8 builds upon this; the fact that God disciplines us shows that we belong to Him. "If you endure chastening [training], God deals with you as with sons; for what son is there whom a father does not chasten? But if you are without chastening [training], of which all have become partakers, then you are illegitimate and not sons."

God's training process makes us more like Him in our character: "Now no chastening [training] seems to be joyful for the present, but grievous; nevertheless, afterward it yields the peaceable fruit of righteousness to those who have been trained by it" (Heb. 12:11). Our gracious God disciplines us so that we can be conformed to His holiness. In the same way, godly fathers train their children through wise discipline, which communicates love, legitimacy, and likeness.

Rearing godly children requires wise admonition, too. An admonition is a verbal warning. God has provided many such warnings to his children in the Bible: "Now all these things [God's multiple judgments upon Israel] happened to them as examples, and they were written for our admonition, on whom the ends of the ages have come" (1 Cor. 10:11).

Paul's two-pronged instruction to the Ephesian saints wasn't a new approach. Consider, for example, Proverbs 29:15: "The rod and reproof give wisdom." For fathers, faith involves taking God at his word and acting upon it.

SPIRIT-FILLED CHILDREN & FATHERS—E

Two application points derive from Ephesians 6:1–4, one of which pertains to children, and the second to fathers. Employment point number one: *Children, obey your parents, which is appropriate.* This is based, of course on Ephesians 6:1 which reads, "Children, obey your parents in the Lord, for this is right." This is as true today as the day it was written, even though we live in a day when biblical standards have been turned on their heads.

In Paul's letter to the church at Rome, he argued that all people are sinners, including children. He listed one of the characteristics of the Fall that pertains to children, namely that they are "disobedient to parents" (Rom. 1:30). Observe how this trait also appears in the Paul's list of last-days sins in his second letter to the young man Timothy: "For men will be lovers of themselves, lovers of money, boasters, proud, blasphemers, disobedient to parents, unthankful, unholy" (2 Tim. 3:2).

I remember when I first learned about this biblical mandate in the Book of Ephesians. I came to Christ at the age of sixteen, and within a year I learned about this principle. Immediately, I began to apply it, doing what was right by obeying my parents. Four years later I can still recall asking my parents—who were in a state of total shock—if I had their permission to marry my Christian girlfriend, Kim. They gladly granted my request. As I look back, I can see how God brought blessing and guidance to my life because I yielded to his governing authorities in my life at that season; my parents.

Children, your assignment commences with yielding your will to God, demonstrated by humbling yourselves under your parents' authority. It is always a step of faith to submit to those God has placed over you in the Lord. Yet if you do it, God will use your mom and dad to give you His direction. Solomon directed many of his proverbs to his son. In one of them he declared, "Trust in the Lord with all your heart, and lean not on your own understanding; In all your ways acknowledge Him, And He shall direct your paths" (Prov. 3:5–6). Specifically, I would like you to honor your parents or guardians by making some kind of sacrifice for them. It can be monetary, by purchasing something for them that would communicate your affection, or you could also make a time sacrifice for them. You could take upon yourself a household chore that they normally would do, and demonstrate how much you cherish them by sacrificing your time.

Dads, it is now your turn. *Fathers, cherish your children through biblical training.* The third employment point reflects how fathers treasure their children by giving them a biblical education. Fathers, as the spiritual head of your home, you must take the baton that God has handed you, and pass it along to the next generation. Remember that Christianity within your family is always one generation away from extinction. In other words, if the faith doesn't get passed down, then it could cease in your family.

Moses understood the importance of a hand-off from fathers to children. He wrote, "And these words which I command you today shall be in your heart; you shall teach them diligently to your children, and shall talk of them when you sit in your house, when you walk by the way, when you lie down, and when your rise up" (Deut. 6:6–7). This sacred charge has been given to fathers specifically. Dads, in all of life, prioritize training your children in God's ways, so that the next generation has an opportunity to represent a strong Christian presence and live long, productive lives. (We know that Billy Joel was wrong when he wrote that only the good die young.)

CHAPTER TWENTY

SERVING HIM WHO BECAME A SERVANT FOR YOU

EPHESIANS 6:5–9

A man told the ringmaster that he was interested in joining the circus as a lion tamer. The ringmaster asked if he had any experience. The man said, "Why, yes. My father was one of the most famous lion tamers in the world, and he taught me everything he knew."

"Really?" said the ringmaster. "Did he teach you how to make a lion jump through a flaming hoop?"

"Yes he did," the man replied.

"And did he teach you how to have six lions form a pyramid?"

"Yes he did," the man replied.

"And have you ever stuck your head in a lion's mouth?"

"Just once," the man replied.

The ringmaster asked, "Why only once?"

The man said, "I was looking for my father."

The first-century world was a dangerous and risky as a lion tamer's. In large cities such as Rome, Ephesus, and Corinth, as much as one-third of the population consisted of slaves. Large numbers of people sold themselves into slavery just to survive. That is why Paul wrote this next part of his letter to the Ephesians, which pertains to Christian slaves and owners:

Servants, be obedient to those who are your masters according to the flesh, with fear and trembling, in sincerity of heart, as to Christ; not with eyeservice, as men-pleasers, but as servants of Christ, doing the will of God from the heart, with good will doing service, as to the Lord, and not to men, knowing that whatever good anyone does, he will receive the same from the Lord, whether he is a slave or free.

And you, masters, do the same things to them, giving up threatening, knowing that your own Master also is in heaven, and there is no partiality with Him.

EPHESIANS 6:5–9, NKJV

Slaves, obey your human masters with fear and trembling, in the sincerity of your heart as to Christ, not like those who do their work only when someone is watching—as people-pleasers—but as slaves of Christ doing the will of God from the heart. Obey with enthusiasm, as though serving the Lord and not people, because you know that each person, whether slave or free, if he does something good, this will be rewarded by the Lord.

Masters, treat your slaves the same way, giving up the use of threats, because you know that both you and they have the same master in heaven, and there is no favoritism with him.

EPHESIANS 6:5–9, NET

SPIRIT-FILLED EMPLOYEES & EMPLOYERS—F

- What is the meaning of the word "servants" (v. 5)?
- Is the word "obedient" used in verse 5 the same Greek word that is applied in Ephesians 6:1 to children?
- What does "eyeservice" mean (v. 6)?
- Is the servant's reward mentioned in verse 8 ("he will receive the same from the Lord") given on earth or in heaven?
- What does Paul mean when he wrote, "And you, masters, do the same thing to them" (v. 9)?

SPIRIT-FILLED EMPLOYEES & EMPLOYERS—I

"Slaves" is the same as the Greek word translated as "servants" in Ephesians

6:5. The term appears 125 times in the Greek New Testament and refers to *one who is in servitude to another.* Slaves had no rights; they solely belonged to their masters. Many of them became Christians. Paul told them, "Be obedient to those who are your masters according the flesh" (v. 5). The imperative, "be obedient," derives from the same verb used in his instructions to children in verse 1; it means *to hear under.*

Slaves were to yield to their earthly masters "with fear and trembling, in sincerity of heart, as to Christ." These bondservants were expected to do more than physical chores. They had the biblical obligation to revere their masters singlemindedly and without duplicity. The Greek word for "sincerity" means *not having an ulterior or double motive.*

Of course this does not apply only to first-century slaves. All labor that takes place in this life should be done for the glory of God, or, as Paul put it in verse 5, "as unto Christ." Martin Luther King summed it up when he wrote: "If it falls your lot to be a street sweeper, sweep streets like Michelangelo painted pictures, sweep streets like Beethoven composed music, sweep streets like Shakespeare wrote poetry. Sweep streets so well that all the hosts of heaven and earth will have to pause and say: Here lived a great street sweeper who swept his job well."

Did you hear about the boss who walked down the hallway into Smith's office and asked, "How long have you been working here, Smith?" Smith replied, "Ever since I heard you walking down the hall, boss." Paul confronted this slothful mentality in verse 6, when he added, "...not with eyeservice, as men-pleasers." "Eyeservice" could literally be translated as "eye slaves." In every time and place, slaves or employees shouldn't just start working when their master or boss emerges to supervise the job, as "menpleasers."

After Paul told the slaves how not to work, he instructed them in how it should be done, "...as servants of Christ, doing the will of God from the heart." As "slaves of Christ," all of our labor should be undertaken for him, and this mindset will enable us to do "the will of God from the heart."

Next Paul dangles the eternal carrot before God's children: "...knowing that whatever good anyone does, he will receive the same from the Lord, whether he is slave or free" (v. 8). Our heavenly Father has an incentive plan for those who labor for Him that is out of this world. Regardless of whether or not you are compensated in this life for your work, you will be rewarded in the life to come—when your work has been done for Jesus!

Paul then turned his attention to Christian masters, "And you, masters, do the same thing to them, giving up threatening, knowing that your own Master also is in heaven, and there is no partiality with Him" (v. 9). The root word for "masters" is often translated "lord" throughout the New Testament. Human lords need to consider the Lord and avoid the trap of exercising authority that is captured in the axiom, "Power corrupts, and absolute power corrupts absolutely."

The masters were "to do the same thing to them," that is, please the Lord by dealing kindly with the slaves. They were to give up threatening and to avoid reflecting the disposition of despots, never menacing their subordinates through intimidation. They should always remember, "Your own Master also is in heaven, and there is no partiality with Him." God's position is greater than the slave owners, and he is always watching them from heaven, judging every person, whether slave or master, by the same standards.

SPIRIT-FILLED EMPLOYEES & EMPLOYERS—R

Paul began this section by addressing slaves, and we know that he identified himself with them. In Romans 1:1, our author called himself "a servant ["slave"] of Jesus Christ." And he was only imitating his Lord Jesus, who voluntarily took on the role of a servant: "Let this mind be in you which was also in Christ Jesus, who, being in the form of God, did not consider it robbery to be equal with God, but made Himself of no reputation, taking the form of a servant ["slave"], and coming in the likeness of men" (Phil. 2:5–7).

Even though the word for "slave" does not appear in John 13 where we read about Jesus washing the disciples feet, clearly he was modeling this attitude for them to follow. Foot-washing was a slave's job in those days of dusty roads, sandaled feet, and reclining on couches at dinner (instead of keeping feet under a table as we do). Who else but a slave would perform such a demeaning task? As the meal was served, Jesus "arose from supper and laid aside His garments, took a towel and girded Himself. After that, He poured water into a basin and began to wash the disciples' feet, and to wipe them with the towel with which He was girded" (John 13:4–6). Needless to say, our Lord did much more than humbly cleanse the feet of his disciples on the eve of his death; he also demonstrated how completely they needed to be willing to lay down their lives one for another, as he was about to do. This is why he said, "For I have given you an example, that you should do as I have done to you" (John 13:15).

What about the masters of the slaves? How should they treat them? God desires all people to be treated with mutual respect since every person—slave or free—has been made in the image of God. Both the Old and New Testaments gave directives concerning the treatment of slaves. Moses wrote, "You shall not rule over them [slaves] with rigor, but you shall fear your God" (Lev. 25:43). In addition, Paul wrote, "Masters, give your servants ["slaves"] what is just and fair, knowing that you also have a Master in heaven" (Col. 4:1).

Unfortunately, as long as civilization exists, people will mistreat each other. Thankfully, this world isn't our home. Christ died to set all men free—spiritually, through salvation, with the expectation of heaven to follow. And as Paul wrote to the members of the church in Galatia, both slave and free: "There is neither Jew nor Greek, there is neither slave nor free, there is neither male nor female; for you are all one in Christ Jesus" (Gal. 3:28).

SPIRIT-FILLED EMPLOYEES & EMPLOYERS—E

Because today in America we don't have institutionalized slavery, I will direct our application points to employees and employers. Our first employment point states: *Employee, work for Jesus and await your reward.*

Have you had some less-than-desirable jobs? Maybe your current work situation is difficult and it seems like your manager graduated from Hades High School. In my two decades of pastoral ministry, I have talked with many church members who were frustrated with their work environment. I joke with my congregation that the reason God gave me a few harsh bosses while I was in the secular work force for twelve years after high school was so that I could sympathize with them. Even today, the tension rises in my gut when someone pours out his or her heart to me because they have a tyrant for a supervisor.

How is it possible to go to work each day with a joyful anticipation knowing that your overseer awaits your arrival just to make you miserable? How did Christian slaves of the first century find the incentive to wake up each day knowing that unsavory jobs awaited, and that they might be rewarded with abuse instead of appreciation for doing the work? The answer is "with Jesus." Consider again Paul's words in verse 5, "Servants, be obedient to those who are your masters according to the flesh, with fear and trembling, in sincerity of heart, as to Christ." We are to learn to work for the only One who can give us an eternal reward, because he will—when the labor is done for Him.

I have a confession to make. I wasn't a hard worker when I entered my first job in 1979. My first occupation was as a typist in a word-processing unit, and the reason I landed the job was because I had taken two typing classes in high school. A couple of years went by, and I attended a Christian seminar that explained the biblical principles of Ephesians 6: 5–8, and I not only learned them but decided to apply them. I started working for the Lord and not for myself.

I still laugh when I think of what my supervisor said when he noticed the obvious change in my work ethic: "Where is Ken and what have you done with him?" Needless to say, by applying *employee, work for Jesus and await your reward,* my life changed drastically for the better.

Employment point number two applies to employers (masters, managers): *Employers, work for Jesus and treat your employees well."* The Golden Rule could apply here. Employers can ask themselves the question, "How would I want to be treated as an employee?" Most likely, anybody who is now in a managerial role worked earlier in his or her carreer as a subordinate.

Paul warned, "Masters, give your servants ["slaves"] what is just and fair, knowing that you also have a Master in heaven" (Col. 4:1). The word "fair" speaks of equality. All people are to be treated with dignity because everyone, employee and boss alike, have been made in the image of God.

CHAPTER TWENTY-ONE

GOT YOUR ARMOR ALL PROTECTANT ON?

EPHESIANS 6:10–24

——∾∾∾——

The second grade teacher said to her class, "The word for today is *fascinate,* and you have to come up with a sentence using that word."

Julie raised her hand, "I went to the zoo and watched the Panda bears on Friday, and it was fascinating."

The teacher responded, "That's nice, but we want to use *fascinate,* not fascinating."

Luke raised his hand, "I went to the rodeo on Saturday and I was fascinated."

The teacher replied, "That's nice, too, but we want to use *fascinate.*"

Timmy extended his hand and declared, "My dad has a shirt with twelve buttons on it, but he's so overweight that he can only *fasten eight.*"

I hope our study of the Book of Ephesians will fascinate you as it has me. The last portion of Paul's letter is all about how we, as children of God, can experience victory over our archenemy, Satan. This is essential battlefield information for every believer:

> Finally, my brethren, be strong in the Lord and in the power of
> His might. Put on the whole armor of God, that you may be able
> to stand against the wiles of the devil. For we do not wrestle against
> flesh and blood, but against principalities, against powers, against
> the rulers of the darkness of this age, against spiritual hosts of
> wickedness in the heavenly places. Therefore take up the whole

armor of God, that you may be able to withstand in the evil day, and having done all, to stand.

Stand therefore, having girded your waist with truth, having put on the breastplate of righteousness, and having shod your feet with the preparation of the gospel of peace; above all, taking the shield of faith with which you will be able to quench all the fiery darts of the wicked one. And take the helmet of salvation, and the sword of the Spirit, which is the word of God; praying always with all prayer and supplication in the Spirit, being watchful to this end with all perseverance and supplication for all the saints— and for me, that utterance may be given to me, that I may open my mouth boldly to make known the mystery of the gospel, for which I am an ambassador in chains; that in it I may speak boldly, as I ought to speak.

But that you also may know my affairs and how I am doing, Tychicus, a beloved brother and faithful minister in the Lord, will make all things known to you; whom I have sent to you for this very purpose, that you may know our affairs, and that he may comfort your hearts. Peace to the brethren, and love with faith, from God the Father and the Lord Jesus Christ. Grace be with all those who love our Lord Jesus Christ in sincerity. Amen.

EPHESIANS 6:10–24, NKJV

Finally, let the mighty strength of the Lord make you strong. Put on all the armor that God gives, so you can defend yourself against the devil's tricks. We are not fighting against humans. We are fighting against forces and authorities and against rulers of darkness and powers in the spiritual world.

So put on all the armor that God gives. Then when that evil day comes, you will be able to defend yourself. And when the battle is over, you will still be standing firm. Be ready! Let the truth be like a belt around your waist, and let God's justice protect you like armor. Your desire to tell the good news about peace should be like shoes on your feet. Let your faith be like a shield, and you will be able to stop all the flaming arrows of the evil one. Let God's saving power be like a helmet, and for a sword use God's message that comes from the Spirit. Never stop praying, especially for others. Always pray by the power of the Spirit. Stay alert and keep praying for God's people. Pray that I will be given the message to speak and that I may fearlessly explain the mystery about the good news. I was sent to do this work, and that's the reason I am in jail. So pray that I will be brave and will speak as I should.

I want you to know how I am getting along and what I am doing. That's why I am sending Tychicus to you. He is a dear friend, as well as a faithful servant of the Lord. He will tell you how I am doing, and he will cheer you up. I pray that God the Father and the Lord Jesus Christ will give peace, love, and faith to every follower! May God be kind to everyone who keeps on loving our Lord Jesus Christ.

EPHESIANS 6:10–24, CEV

HOW TO OVERCOME THE SPIRITUAL MAFIA—F

- Why does Paul use the word "finally" (Eph. 6:10)?
- Where does Paul get his imagery for the "armor of God?"
- What does the word "wiles" mean (Eph. 6:11)?
- Who are the "spiritual hosts of wickedness in the heavenly places" (Eph. 6:12)?
- When is "the evil day" (Eph. 6:13)?
- What do the various pieces of armor represent in Ephesians 6:14–17?
- Is "praying always," mentioned in Eph. 6:18 a part of the armor that Paul refers to in verses 14–17?
- What role did Tychicus have from Paul and to the Ephesian church?

HOW TO OVERCOME THE SPIRITUAL MAFIA—I

Paul introduced the concluding part of his letter with the word, "Finally" and then added the command, "be strong in the Lord, and in the power of His might" (v. 10). A second command appears in the next verse: "Put on the whole armor of God." Where did Paul obtain the imagery of armor? I believe it came from the fact that his imprisonment consisted of a house arrest and being chained to a Roman soldier (see Ephesians 6:20). He had plenty of time to contemplate a Roman soldier's complete armor, which would have comprised a shield, sword, lance, helmet, greaves, and breast-plate. Although Paul didn't give every piece of armor a spiritual counterpart in the passage, he wanted to show how the Ephesian believers could be totally protected from "the wiles of the devil." The theme of *standing firm* occurs four times within this short text with the purpose of exhorting them to withstand in victory over the methods (the literal meaning of "wiles") of the wicked one.

Satan cannot be everywhere at once; therefore, he has organized his demons, who are fallen angels, to carry out his dastardly deeds. I refer to this hierarchy as the spiritual mafia. Paul wrote, "For we do not wrestle against flesh and blood"(v. 12) to show the diabolical nature of these unseen forces. Just because they are invisible for the most part doesn't mean that believers should minimize these opponents. To show the fierce conflict, Paul carefully chose the term "wrestle" that was used outside of the religious context in the worlds of athletic wrestling and military hand-to-hand com-bat. Only by donning a complete suit of spiritual armor as supplied by God and by actively fighting a Christian experience sustained victory over these invisible enemy forces.

It is "on account of this" demonic combat that Paul then gave for the second time the command, "Take up the whole armor of God" (v. 13). He used the terms, "put on" and "take up" to denote an action that was under-taken once and for all. These verbs speak of a decisive act of the will.

In other words, Christian soldiers, wear your armor continually, "that you may be able to withstand in the evil day, and having done all, to stand" (v. 13). What is "the evil day"? It is when you encounter the Dragon's breath in your life, the moment of temptation. It can be an intense wrestling match. However, we don't fight as much *for* victory as we do *from* victory––thanks to Jesus Christ, who has defeated both the Devil and death.

Paul began verse 14 with another command, "Stand therefore, having girded your waist with truth." The soldier was first to have his belt tightly tied around his waist. This sent a message to everyone that the he was alert and on duty; a loosened belt signified that he was off the clock. The "belt" or "girdle" with which he girded himself held all of his equipment together, including his sword. This is why the apostle described truth as essential for every soldier of Christ.

Next Paul depicted another vital piece of protection, "having put on the breastplate of righteousness" (v. 14b). Usually made of bronze, a Roman breastplate covered the body from the neck to the thighs and consisted of two parts to protect the warrior's front and back; it protected the heart. When Christians have on their breastplate of righteousness, they have put on the protection of the divine righteousness that Jesus won for them and gave them at their salvation.

Moving on, Paul exhorted the brethren to pull onto their feet "the preparation of the gospel of peace" (v. 15). The Jewish historian Flavius Josephus described Roman military footware as thickly studded with sharp nails, which kept them from falling in the midst of a skirmish. The continued proclamation of the gospel brings stable footing and peace to the Christian soldier.

Paul added, in Ephesians 6:16, "Above all, taking the shield of faith with which you will be able to quench all the fiery darts of the wicked one." The Greek word for "shield" originally referred to a door or gate for closing a cave. Later this term pointed to a shield that had the shape of a door. It was approximately four feet long and two-and-a-half feet wide. The shields could interlock and consisted of two layers of wood glued together, covered with linen and hide and bound with iron.

The shield's protective value cannot be minimized. When the hosts of hell launch their attacks, "the shield of faith" repels them.

Next, "and take the helmet of salvation" (v. 17). To "take" means to welcome the gift of salvation and its outworking. Salvation ensures that the child of God will have right thinking, which is another way of talking about the safety of the head.

Last, but certainly not least, the child of God must carry the only offensive weapon mentioned in this section of Scripture, "the sword of the Spirit, which is the word of God" (v. 17b). The spoken Word of God powerfully protects and enables God's warrior to fight through the onslaughts of the Prince of Darkness. Paul's advice: "Don't leave home without it."

Paul wants Christians to secure their armor to prayer: "Praying always with all prayer and supplication in the Spirit, being watchful to this end with all perseverance and supplication for all the saints" (v. 18). As Paul exhorted the saints to pray on behalf of one another, he also requested their intercession so that he might confidently proclaim Jesus as his "ambassador in chains" (vv. 19–20).

Paul had his own ambassador, Tychicus, who carried this letter to the Ephesians and gave them an update on his own condition (vv. 21–22). He finished this inspired epistle with this blessing to his children in the faith: "Peace to the brethren, and love with faith, from God the Father and the Lord Jesus Christ. Grace be with all those who love our Lord Jesus Christ in sincerity. Amen."

HOW TO OVERCOME THE SPIRITUAL MAFIA—R

In order for you as a child of God to "be strong in the Lord and in the power of His might," you must first believe that God is who he says he is, and then claim his promises as Abraham did: "He did not waver at the promise of God through unbelief, but was strengthened in the faith, giving glory to God" (Rom. 4:20). As Abraham trusted that God could make of him a mighty nation, the soldier of the Lord must depend upon the Father's grace in the heat of battle. In the context of being a "good soldier," Paul told Timothy: "You therefore, my son, be strong in the grace that is in Christ Jesus" (2 Tim. 2:1).

In order to fight as a soldier of Christ, you have to arise from your seat. Four times Paul told the Ephesians to "stand" (vv. 11, 13, 14), or to "withstand" (v. 13). Being in an upright position puts the child of God on full alert "against the wiles of the devil." The word "wiles" implies the shrewdness of Satan and a savvy warrior understands the tactics of the wicked one, "for we are not ignorant of his devices" (2 Cor. 2:11). Having the opponent's playbook helps us to know what seductions Satan will hurl at us next. Since Satan isn't ubiquitous (everywhere at once), he assigns his hit squad, the spiritual mafia (his demons), to lure and entrap people with "the lust of the flesh" and "the lust of the eyes" and "the pride of life" (1 John 2:15–16).

Paul wrote, "Stand therefore, having girded your waist with truth" (v. 14) because Satan is a master deceiver and the father of lies (John 8:44). Our spiritual growth and protection from him comes from abiding in truth. Paul showed this earlier in Ephesians 4:15—"but, speaking the truth in love, may [you] grow up in all things into Him who is the head—Christ." From the Messiah, Jesus Christ, came these prayerful words to the Father, "Sanctify them by Your truth. Your word is truth" (John 17:17).

Don't minimize the maliciousness of the Devil. "Be sober, be vigilant; because your adversary the devil walks about like a roaring lion, seeking whom he may devour. Resist him, steadfast in the faith, knowing that the same sufferings are experienced by your brotherhood in the world" (1 Pet. 5:8–9). The "shield of faith" gives cover from Satan's attacks and also shows the safety of Christian unity. Roman soldiers while marching side-by-side could interlock their shields and demonstrate a joint show of might. Truly there is safety in numbers, but also in the cohesiveness of God's children marching together with linked shields. Remember that Paul had earlier exhorted the Ephesians "to have a walk worthy of the calling with which you were called, with all lowliness and gentleness, with longsuffering, bearing with one another in love, endeavoring to keep the unity of the Spirit in the bond of peace" (Eph. 4:1–3). No Christian will thrive with a Lone Ranger mentality.

Every Roman soldier understood the importance not only of protection but also of engaging the enemy. Jesus masterfully wielded the sword of the spirit (the Word of God) during his attacks from Satan. He quoted Deuteronomy 8:3 to overcome the enemy's temptation in the wilderness: "It is written, 'Man shall not live by bread alone, but by every word that proceeds from the mouth of God'" (Matt. 4:4). In the thick of the battle, don't keep your sword in its scabbard. Use it unsparingly!

Prayer binds together the Christian soldier's armor. The simplified formula occurs in 1 Thessalonians 5:17, "Pray without ceasing." What breath is to physical life, prayer is for spiritual life. Prayer shows complete dependence upon God and also boldness. Peter and John shamelessly proclaimed Jesus. The Sanhedrin tried to intimidate them not to preach the gospel. What enabled these greatly persecuted apostles to keep on proclaiming the good news when their lives were in jeopardy? Prayer. "And when they had prayed, the place where they were assembled together was shaken; and they were all filled with the Holy Spirit, and they spoke the word of God with boldness" (Acts 4:31).

HOW TO OVERCOME THE SPIRITUAL MAFIA—E

As Paul instructed Timothy, "All Scripture is given by inspiration of God and is profitable..." (2 Tim. 3:16). The entire Bible gives us beneficial information and helps us to mature spiritually. Yet some portions of the Word seem to have greater relevance than others. The employment of the armor of God is one of those sections. Without the armor of God, the saints are ineffective against the prince of darkness.

Apply the following three points from Ephesians 6:10–20 to keep experiencing regular triumph over Satan. (1) *Be powerful by putting on God's armor;* (2) *Be protected by wearing God's armor;* (3) *Be prayerful with petitions by God's Spirit.* Allow your indwelling Advocate, the Holy Spirit, to move you to prayer continuously. Jesus introduced a parable in Luke 18:1 with these words, "that men always ought to pray and not lose heart." Couple this with our Lord's warning to his drowsy disciples in Gethsemane, "Watch and pray, lest your enter into temptation. The spirit indeed is willing, but the flesh is weak" (Matt. 26:41).

To close out this most important portion of Scripture, and all that we've covered together from the profound Word of God, I will leave you with the words of Charles Wesley's hymn, *Soldiers of Christ Arise:*

Soldiers of Christ arise, and put your armor on,
strong in the strength which God supplies through his eternal Son;
strong in the Lord of Hosts, and in his mighty power,
who in the strength of Jesus trusts is more than conqueror.

Stand then in his great might, with all his strength endued,
but take, to arm you for the fight, the panoply of God;
that having all things done, and all your conflicts passed,
ye may o'ercome thru Christ alone and stand entire at last.

Leave no unguarded place, no weakness of the soul,
Take every virtue, every grace, and fortify the whole.
From strength to strength go on, wrestle and fight and pray,
Tread all the pow'rs of darkness down and win the well-fought day.

NOTES

CHAPTER ONE
PAUL'S APOSTOLIC TIDINGS

1. As found at preachingtoday.com (http://www.preachingtoday.com/illustrations/2000/june/12467.html), from Bill Bright, *How to be Filled with the Spirit.*

CHAPTER TWO
THREE REASONS WHY YOU SHOULD BLESS GOD

1. Chuck Swindoll, *Elijah: A Man of Heroism and Humility* (Nashville: Word, 2000), 121–122.

CHAPTER SIX
WHY DID GOD PERFORM THE ULTIMATE DEAD LIFT?

1. As found at http://www.preachingtoday.com/illustration/2007/may

CHAPTER ELEVEN
WHAT'S THE PURPOSE FOR BIBLICAL FOLLOW-THE-LEADER?

1. As found at preachingtoday.com/illustration/2005/july

CONNECT WITH THE AUTHOR
Website: colmarmanorbible.org
Email: colmarmanorbiblechurch@comcast.net

CPSIA information can be obtained at www.ICGtesting.com
Printed in the USA
BVOW03s1818230415

397478BV00006B/32/P